Russia and The World:

A Study of the War and a Statement of the World-problems that now confront Russia and Great Britain. ❧ With Illustrations from Original Photographs. By STEPHEN GRAHAM ❧ ❧

❧

CASSELL AND COMPANY, LTD
London, Toronto and Melbourne
1915

First Published . . . . *February* 1915
Reprinted . . . . *February* 1915
Reprinted . . . . *March* 1915
Reprinted . . . . *April* 1915

Preface

IN December, 1913, when I was just returning to Russia after my tramp in America, *The Times* came forward and put its columns at my disposal, and I was able to record my impressions there throughout the whole of the year. During the winter I was seeking words and stories and impressions that would convey better the idea of Russia as the great religious force of Europe: Russia the sanctuary from Westernism, Americanism, and the materialism of the age. My first articles dealt with the religion of Russia, the meeting of old friends, the idea of sanctuary. I visited friends of long standing, whom I have written in my books—Pereplotchikof, the Russian painter, with whom I spent a summer in the forests of. Archangel; Loosha, whom I met at Batum; Varvara Ilinitchna of the cottage with the Chinese wall at Gelendzhik, on the Black Sea shore; the old grandmother at Vladikavkaz, to whom I brought a crown of thorns and a cross after my pilgrimage to Jerusalem. My first letters home were from Moscow, Kief, Vladikavkaz, and other towns.

But with the coming of spring the road tempted me, and I set out on the longest and most difficult tramp I had yet attempted — across Russian Central Asia to the frontier of China and the south of Central Siberia. I went by train as far as the road would take me, and then went on with pack on back. I visited Bokhara, Samarkand, and Tashkent, those wondrous cities which Russia possesses on the northern side of Afghanistan and the Hindu-Koosh. Towards the end of May I set out across the Kirghiz steppes, through Sirdaria and Seven Rivers Land, and saw many scores of new Russian villages and irrigated farms in this the youngest of Russian colonies. I was continually with the pioneers of Russian emigration —the endless caravan of ox-drawn or pony-drawn carts carrying all the goods and families of Russians going to the remote East in search of land. It was an interesting tramp, but very hot, very trying. The sun beat down on the desert, and for days there was never a tree, not even a palm tree, under which to shelter. It is a land full of big game, many tigers, many panthers, antelope, maral. There are many serpents, many eagles and vultures and huge bustards. There are also myriads of creatures of the desert—tortoises, marmottes, dust beetles.

I reached the posts of what is nominally the boundary line of China, and passed through many Cossack settlements by Kopal, Lepsinsk, and Lake Maiman to Semipalatinsk. At Semipalatinsk, where, by the by, Dostoieffsky suffered part of his exile to Siberia, I came into touch with civilisation, received a stack of letters and newspapers, among other things read of the assassination of the Archduke Ferdinand and his bride and of the consequent punitive expedition of the Austrians. It seemed a serious matter to me then, and I wondered whether things might not be more interesting to me if I returned to the more western parts of Russia, but I was loth to forgo the prospect of resting through late July and August in the Altai—those magnificent pine-covered snow-crested mountains that divide Siberia from China, and give birth to those wondrous rivers of Asia, the Irtish and the Yenisei. I went south to Malo-Krasnoyark, and then alongside the main Altai range and over the green hills up to the high-lands of Katun Karagai. And there, whilst living in a Cossack station, I heard the barely credible intelligence that there was war.

No one could say with whom there was war, but there certainly was war with someone. It was a terrible moment when I heard that Germany had declared war on Russia, but it was tempered by the fact that I could hardly believe the news to be true. Still, with the call to arms, my vagabondage in Central Asia came to an end for the time being. So the war came across my little thread of life.

This book takes up my story on the day of mobilisa-tion on the Altai Mountains. At first I thought of in-cluding the whole of the year's experience and thought and impressions of my Central Asian journey in one book with my pictures and thoughts of the war. But I have put aside the earlier matter, as hardly relevant to the immediate question of how the war is affecting Russia and how Russia stands in relation to the nations she pro-tects and to the world in general. Some time later I hope to return to the Altai village and resume my wanderings where I left off, and, when I have crossed Siberia, may perhaps present a personal impression of the Russian Empire.

In regard to the spelling of Russian and Polish names, I have kept to the rule of spelling according to sound. It would be well if the Press as a whole would spell according to sound, and Przemysl became simply Pshemisl, and Czestochowa simply Chenstokhof as they are pronounced, and so on.

S. G.

February, 1915.

Contents

War

Contents

Policies–continued

Last Thoughts

Illustrations

War

RUSSIA AND THE WORLD

HOW THE NEWS OF WAR CAME TO A VILLAGE ON THE CHINESE FRONTIER

I WAS staying in an Altai Cossack village on the frontier of Mongolia when the war broke out, 1,200 versts south of the Siberian railway, a most verdant resting-place with majestic fir forests, snow-crowned mountains range behind range, green and purple valleys deep in larkspur and monkshood. All the young men and women of the village were out on the grassy hills with scythes; the children gathered currants in the wood each day, old folks sat at home and sewed furs together, the pitch-boilers and charcoal-burners worked at their black fires with barrels and scoops, and athwart it all came the message of war.

At 4 a.m. on July 31st the first telegram came through; an order to mobilise and be prepared for active service. I was awakened that morning by an unusual commotion, and, going into the village street, saw the soldier population collected in groups, talking excitedly. My peasant hostess cried out to me, "Have you heard the news? There is war." A young man on a fine horse came galloping down the street, a great red flag hanging from his shoulders and flapping in the wind, and as he went he called out the news to each and every one, "War! War!"

Russia and the World

Horses out, uniforms, swords! The village *feldscher* took his stand outside our one Government building, the *volostnoe pravlenie*, and began to examine horses. The Tsar had called on the Cossacks; they gave up their work without a regret and burned to fight the enemy.

Who was the enemy? Nobody knew. The telegram contained no indications. All the village population knew was that the same telegram had come as came ten years ago, when they were called to fight the Japanese. Rumours abounded. All the morning it was persisted that the yellow peril had matured, and that the war was with China. Russia had pushed too far into Mongolia, and China had declared war.

The village priest, who spoke Esperanto and claimed that he had never met anyone else in the world who spoke the language, came to me and said:

"What think you of Kaiser William's picture?"

"What do you mean?" I asked.

"Why, the yellow peril!"

Then a rumour went round, "It is with England, with England." So far away these people lived they did not know that our old hostility had vanished. Only after four days did something like the truth come to us, and then nobody believed it.

"An immense war," said a peasant to me. "Thirteen powers engaged—England, France, Russia, Belgium, Bulgaria, Servia, Montenegro, Albania, against Germany, Austria, Italy, Roumania, Turkey."

Two days after the first telegram a second came, and this one called up every man between the ages of eighteen and forty-three. Astonishing that Russia should at the very outset begin to mobilise its reservists 5,000 versts from the scene of hostilities!

The Cossacks Mobilise

Flying messengers arrived on horses, breathless and steaming, and delivered packets into the hands of the *Ataman*, the head-man of the Cossacks—the secret instructions. Fresh horses were at once given them, and they were off again within five minutes of their arrival in the village. The great red flag was mounted on an immense pine-pole at the end of our one street, and at night it was taken down and a large red lantern was hung in its place. At the entrance of every village such a flag flew by day, such a lantern glowed by night.

The preparations for departure went on each day, and I spent much time watching the village vet. certifying or rejecting mounts. A horse that could not go fifty miles a day was not passed. Each Cossack brought his horse up, plucked its lips apart to show the teeth, explained marks on the horse's body, mounted it bareback and showed its paces. The examination was strict; the Cossacks had a thousand miles to go to get to the railway at Omsk. It was necessary to have strong horses.

On the Saturday night there was a melancholy service in the wooden village church. The priest, in a long sermon, looked back over the history of Holy Russia, dwelling chiefly on the occasion when Napoleon defiled the churches of "Old Mother Moscow," and was punished by God. "God is with us," said the priest. "Victory will be ours."

Sunday was a holiday, and no preparations were made that day. On Monday the examination of horses went on. The Cossacks brought also their uniforms, swords, hats, half-shubas, overcoats, shirts, boots, belts—all that they were supposed to provide in the way of kit, and the *Ataman* checked and certified each soldier's portion.

5

Russia and the World

On Thursday, the day of setting out, there came a third telegram from St. Petersburg. The vodka-shop, which had been locked and sealed during the great temperance struggle which had been in progress in Russia, might be opened for one day only—the day of mobilisation. After that day, however, it was to be closed again and remain closed until further orders.

What scenes there were that day!

All the men of the village had become soldiers and pranced on their horses. At eight o'clock in the morning the holy-water basin was taken from the church and placed with triple candles on the open, sun-blazed mountain side. The Cossacks met there as at a rendezvous, and all their women-folk, in multifarious bright cotton dresses and tear-stained faces, walked out to say a last religious good-bye.

The bare-headed, long-haired priest came out in vestment of violent blue, and behind him came the old men of the village carrying the ikons and banners of the church; after them the village choir, singing as they marched. A strange mingling of sobbing and singing went up to heaven from the crowd outside the wooden village, this vast irregular collection of women on foot clustered about a long double line of stalwart horsemen.

The consecration service took place, and only then did we learn the almost incredible fact that the war was with Germany. It made the hour and the act and the place even more poignant. I at least understood what it meant to go to war against Germany, and the destiny that was in store.

"God is with you," said the priest in his sermon,

Cossack bringing his fur coat to the revision of kit.

the tears running down his face the while. "God is with you; not a hair of your heads will be lost. Never turn your backs on the foe. Remember that if you do, you endanger the eternal welfare of your souls. Remember, too, that a letter, a post card—one line—will be greedily read by all of us who remain behind. . . . God bless His faithful slaves!"

When the lesson was read there was a great scramble among the soldiers to get their heads underneath the Bible. They looked true "slaves of God," these soldiers on their knees in the blazing sunlight, the great Bible on their very heads.

Each soldier dismounted and prostrated himself in the prayers; each soldier at the last kissed the Cross in the priest's hand, and was anointed on the brow with holy water.

And when anointed he passed away from the priest, leading his horse by the bridle. He sought out mother and wife in the waiting throng, embraced them, and was blessed amidst sobbings that wrung the heart.

"They'll be back soon!" says one woman.

"Oh, you don't know, you don't know," replies another in distraction.

Away! Away! Two miles from the village an ox had been killed and was being cooked by the side of the road, and gallon bottles of vodka waited in the grass. The soldiers got into saddle again and rode out through the crowds of women, old men, and children. And a great number followed them to the place of picnic.

The ox was cooked over a great fire by the riverside, the green birches withering in the smoke. The Cossacks came up quickly, and getting down from their horses tied them to the trees.   Buckets and kettles and glasses were brought forth from a shed, also many plates, but no tables.   There was soup and roast beef and vodka for all comers.   First of all the gallon bottles of spirit were emptied into the buckets and kettles and distributed among the men, the men themselves officiating.   There were drinks all round, and healths to the Tsar, and to Russia, and to themselves.   Whilst the vodka was being thus purveyed, the cauldrons were receiving attention, and directly the toasts were drunk the soup was dealt out, each man holding his plate as he stood and putting his lips to the hot liquid, blowing it, and trying to drink it; there were no spoons.   Meat was carved and taken promiscuously to eat, and then the vodka was finished.   Only a very limited quantity had been supplied, but enough to inflame the emotionalised souls of men so lately taken through a moving religious ceremony, so lately touched to tears by the farewell to home.

One man held up a rouble, showing the Emperor's face, and all the soldiers sang " God Save the Tsar," and then danced round the coin.

The *Ataman* was taken, hoisted shoulder-high, and thrown three times into the air, and caught again with cheers — a great, stout, bearded military official.   A number of soldiers even came up to me and laid their hands on me, saying,—"*Pozvoltye Vas raskatchat—*Let's give you a swing."

I had difficulty in getting away.

.   .   .   .   .   .

The roaring little river rushed along under the birch trees, the horses waited in the green shade, the men danced and sang, the women sobbed and keened.

8

Wives of the Cossacks

There was an hour of it, and then the officer in command gave the word, and all the men were in the stirrup again. The long journey and farewell began in earnest. Even so, women on horseback accompanied their husbands twenty or thirty miles and then said good-bye, and even watched them out of sight as they dipped with their dust into the horizon.

So Russia sent off her men from the frontier of Mongolia to fight on the far-off plains of Austria and Poland.

THE JOURNEY FROM THE ALTAI
MOUNTAINS TO MOSCOW

THE day after the setting out of the Cossacks from their Altai village on the Mongolian frontier I decided to follow — hiring first the post and then the *zemsky* horses. It was like following a reaping. Wherever I went all the able-bodied men had gone before me ; there were only old men, women and children remaining. Boys of twelve and thirteen were in charge of the Government horses, women who could neither read nor write had charge of the post-stations. Grey-beards worked with girls in the haymaking fields. Outside every village still hung by day the red flag of war ; by night, the great red lantern with baleful light.

A fine journey along the corridors of the Altai ranges, from settlement to settlement, through prairie grass, a warm wind blowing all the day, a golden moon coming up out of China to rule in the night. The heart trembled at the thought of war, but all around was the indifferent peace of a remote country. It was tantalising to look at this glowing Altai moon, so placid and perfect, and to feel that four thousand miles away the destinies of Europe were being settled on the field of battle.

How slow was my progress. After four days I got on a river steamer, packed with reservists, and started the long river journey down the Irtish to Semipalatinsk and Omsk. The cabins of the boat were occupied by officers, the deck by the soldiers, and civil passengers of whatever description were put in the holds with the cargo, the men fore, the women aft. Doctors, peasants, engineers, fishermen, Civil servants, farmers, found themselves cheek by cheek and knee by knee, trying to sleep on sacks of rye and trusses of hay. But there was no grumbling; everyone understood that it was "soldiers first."

We stayed all night at Ust-Kamenygorsk. There was a hurricane of wind and drenching rain. No one on board the ship slept, but all sat and looked serious, while soldiers stood about in their cloaks, and the pale lights of the ship shimmered on black bayonets. Next morning we were played off by a military band. There was a crowd as if the whole female population of the town had come out to see us off; and as the National Anthem was played the sobs of mothers and wives mingled in unison with the music as we beat the water into foam and steamed away.

All the way to Semipalatinsk the women came out from the villages and lined the riverside to see us— not to sell things, as in time of peace, but to give. We stopped nowhere, but glided gently by the village landing-places; and as we did so the women flung aboard their gifts to the soldiers—5lb. loaves, cucumbers, red melons, cooked fish—crying and shouting the while. Many loaves and fishes had adventurous passages in their flight from the shore to the boat. How good that this personal sort of charity is still deep in Russia, not dried up! In the old days when the Siberian prisoners were marched from village to village to the mines the population of the villages used to turn out and befriend them in just such a way. To-day in Moscow I see how the people of the towns wait at the stations for the ambulance trains and carry their gifts to the captive and wounded—personally. Even to the German prisoners of war.

There was a great deal of feasting and merriment on board the boat, though no vodka or beer. The stove in the general kitchen was always covered with pots, and in the pots were fish, eggs, chickens, mutton. There was eating and talking, and music and dancing. When at Semipalatinsk we were transferred to the much larger steamer *Andrew the First-Called*, there was dancing all night.

On the deck of the *Andrew the First-Called* we had a thousand passengers, half of whom were reservists, the other half a medley of delayed Siberian passengers : Chinamen on the way to Peking, Chinese Tartars, Siberian Tartars, gangs of labourers, colonists, school-teachers going home from their holiday in the Altai, students going to the universities, a party of Caucasian pioneers returning to Alagir, near Vladikavkaz ; five Ossetine tribesmen, who, strange to say, had been in Canada and who spoke broken English, and were of opinion that Siberia was "no good country"; a family of Ziriani going back to their home on the Petchora. In every corner and on every table rolled canteloupes and mush melons, giving colours of gold and emerald to the monotony of Siberian rags. We were a long-haired, non-shaven lot of people. I myself had a month's hair on my face. We were in bark boots, in jackboots, in bare and dirty feet. We had many "hares" on board —ticketless passengers, tramps, tatterdemalions, men of the runaway convict type, beggars, thieves.

I lay in the midst of them all and slept not. An orchestra was formed of two men with concertinas, three with fiddles, and one with a mouth organ, and even at three in the morning the musicians were surrounded by a great crowd of men; some on sacks, some standing on benches and tables, some hanging on from rafters in the roof above, cheering, shouting, singing, as men couples went through the extraordinary dumb show of the popular dances, coming towards one another or retiring, averting their faces, shrugging their shoulders, hunching their backs, slipping down, and dancing as it were on hips and heels, springing up again, kissing one another on the lips.

Besides myself there was another Englishman on board, a mining expert who had come down from one of the mines which used to be worked by the convicts, but which a British company is now exploiting. Five hundred of his labourers had been taken away for the war; the mines would perhaps have to close down. The company's stock must have depreciated fifty per cent. It was the same with all the other mining concerns. The Englishman, however, was cheerful. Optimism had always carried him through. He was still an optimist. By the time we got to Omsk it would be arbitration. "Arbitration," said he, "that's what it will be." A Russian officer, overhearing our talk and learning that we were English, lifted his hat to us.

What animation there was at Omsk; soldiers galloping about or leading horses to and from the river, great companies of reservists in rags, free dining-places for reservists' families, companies of soldiers in new attire and with new rifles, squads of men drilling on the sands, train after train packed with soldiers, all the red Siberian goods trucks emptied of the merchandise of peace, and full of guns, saddles, oats, hay; laden with military carts and wagons, with soldiers and horses!

I was appreciably nearer the war, but still far away. The railway line was blocked for passenger service, and it was only in the slowest, slowest manner that I made the 2,000-mile journey west to Moscow, passing through the endless forests of Tobolsk, Perm, Viatka, Kostroma, Vologda, tasting the sodden stillness of the pine woods, picking up little contingents of reservists at village stations, listening to the sobbing of women saying "good-bye," watching military goods trains go past us, waiting hours, waiting whole nights to go on, the only diversion the telegrams for sale at the railway stations, the news of the doings of the armies.

THE ENGLISHMAN

THE Englishman with whom I came from the Altai was an interesting character. I met him at Semipalatinsk, the miserable sandswept Siberian town where, for many years, Dostoieffsky was confined. I was wandering from the quay up to the town hoping to get a current newspaper to read, when suddenly, to my surprise, a man in a cart cried out to me in my own tongue the words : "Speak English ? "

" Why, yes," said I. "How did you guess ? "

" I saw you reading an old copy of *The Times* yesterday, but I thought probably you didn't really know much and it wouldn't be worth while speaking to you."

" You were on the *Mongol ?* "

" Yes, I got in at Ust-Kamenygorsk coming down from a mine."

" I suppose you know the news—England has declared war also."

" What ! Is she at it ? "

" Yes, it's England, France and Russia against Germany and Austria."

" No. But it won't last."

" There's no going home across Germany."

" No ? "

" I don't suppose there's any sailing from Baltic ports."

"No. But it can't last. It'll be arbitration."

The mining engineer seemed perturbed. I went on

to the town; he returned to the boat after a night in a hotel. We met later on the *Andrew the First-Called* and we had many talks. A very able man of middle years, at once prosaic and sentimental, having soft blue eyes ready to shed tears, faded hair and heavyish body. He was home-sick for England, and talked ever of his wife and his little girl living in a cosy home in one of our western seaports.

> "Falmouth is a fine town with ships in the bay,
> And I wish from my heart it was there I was to-day.
> I wish from my heart I was far away from here,
> Sitting in my parlour and talking to my dear."

Yet the stirring scenes of the Russian mobilisation and the sobbing of the women touched him, and he told me that up country he had seen sights no man could face unmoved.

His first feeling about the war and England's part in it was irritation, but as I read him extracts from the sheaves of Government telegrams I had procured at Semipalatinsk Town Hall, he was moved with the spirit of adventure, and he told me of many things that had happened to him whilst prospecting in Nigeria and Ashanti; how he discovered a cliff of anthracite and wanted to take up an option on the working of it, but the Government forestalled him; how he was once reported dead, and came home to read his obituary notice and find his wife in black.

He held that the Russian Empire was stronger than the British Empire because of the lack of education in Russia. Education always made for disintegration. The educated man nearly always wanted to sacrifice something else to himself and his own education. He was not ready to make sacrifices for a larger ideal.

The Gospel of Optimism

But the engineer believed in the English, especially in contrast with Americans. The Americans always think they can outdo other people by hustling. He told me how up at the mine there were two Americans who tried "to get a move on the labourers" by showing an example and taking pick and shovel themselves.

"The men all stood round and laughed and let the Americans work. No, the way to get Kirghiz and Russians to work is to make a game of it, and knock a man's hat off now and then and joke about it."

A cheerful, optimistic Briton. Once he lost £12,000 on an investment in American rails and he felt very down in spirits.

"I might have saved £8,500 by selling out when I wanted to, but my broker said 'Hold on till morning and you'll double.' Next morning I was broke. I did not let my wife know. I went about London all day miserable. I always occupy the same room at the Cecil. In the evening I went along to the Gaiety Theatre. I sat in the stalls and stared at the piece, but couldn't take it in, I was so upset by the money I'd lost. After the show I met an old acquaintance who asked me into Romano's for supper. There by chance I met Edmund Payne, Gertie Millar, her husband and some others. Gertie Millar asked me how I liked the piece. I replied that it seemed pretty good, but my mind was wandering all the time.

"'Why, what's the matter?' said she, and she looked at me so kindly and seriously I could see she understood, and she put her hand on my knee and said words that I shall never forget:—

'Laugh, and the world laughs with you ;
Weep, and you weep alone.'

Russia and the World

"Next day I won £1,500 back on a thousand pound margin on Ashantis.

"So I say it'll be arbitration. I shall get home from St. Petersburg in three days, through the Kiel Canal. Have you ever seen the canal? No? You ought to. I've only seen it once and that was at night. But I stayed up all night looking at it. It's a magnificent piece of engineering."

| IN MOSCOW

THERE is one characteristic in the life of a young man; it is that no matter what happens, good results to him thereby: Luck, so-called, is much more on the side of the young man than on the side of the old. What hairbreadth escapes he has, what calamities he faces, what hardships he undergoes. Yet he emerges more powerful, more experienced. Indeed, danger and privation are more beneficial to him than peace and happiness. Russia is for the moment our young man, with all his destiny before him. He has come through the Japanese War, the great revolutionary danger, he is now in the depths of his third and greatest struggle. All goes to the making of mighty Russia.

So, when I got back to Moscow in September, 1914, I found no depression of the national spirit in Russia; no strikes, no riots, no revolutionary propaganda or pessimism, but instead an all-pervading cheerfulness and national unanimity which even the most optimistic could not have foreseen. The peasants go to the front with great enthusiasm; and the *intelligentsia*, Radical and Conservative alike, cheer them on. The newspapers of all parties are at one, and the Liberal organs are as loyal as those of the extreme Right. There is the same unanimity among the Poles and the Jews—volunteer regiments have even been formed. The only coldness towards Russia lies in the breasts of the Finns; the only instinct to fall into brigandage and rebellion is among the Mohammedan tribesmen of the Caucasus. All is well, and if success crowns the Russian arms, the empire will become bound in happy allegiance to the Tsar as never before. On the other hand, if the Germans gain the ascendant, and inflict vast slaughter, the presence of millions of armed Russians in Western Russia is pregnant with danger for all who have property and culture and position there. This war is a matter of life and death for Russian civilisation, as it is for all the other States engaged.

The air is full of hope. All vodka shops have been closed, and Russia at a word from the Tsar has taken on the appearance of sobriety. It has been impossible to obtain alcoholic liquors of any kind, and as a consequence drunkenness has disappeared from the streets, and with it a great army of beggars who only beg that they may gather twenty kopeks for a bottle. The absence of vodka made a great blank in the peasants' lives, but that blank has been filled up by the war and the interest of the war. Ordinarily the peasants feel they have nothing to do but drink, but now it is otherwise. It is as if in war they found a real reason for existence, as if in death they found the object of living. It is difficult to reconcile war with our Western Christianity, but the Church of Russia finds no difficulty—going to the war is laying one's body on the altar of sacrifice. In the fine rage of the Russian soldiers going to meet the foe lies the thrill of exultation in the souls of martyrs going to a glorious death.

My ears ache with the sound of women's sobs. All the way from the peaceful and happy villages of the Altai the sounds of wailing and crying broke upon my ears. Here, however, in Moscow it is different: some-

Love for the Soldiers

one has wiped away their tears, and the women with sunshiny, if tear-stained, faces are feverishly working for the thousands of wounded who have come back for their care, cutting linen and sewing bandages, collecting money, organising hospitals. There are many wounded in Moscow. All the public hospitals and infirmaries are filled, all the private hospitals. Scores of large private houses, such as that of Prince Gagarin, on the Novinsky Boulevard, and Mme. Morozof's, on the Vozdvizhenka, are turned into *lazaretti*—honeycombs of nursing chambers and beds ; or into linen warehouses or workshops for bandage cutting and rolling. The streets are thronged with Red Cross sisters; in every house women are thinking what they can do personally for the wounded, how many they can take to nurse. Alas ! we are only at the beginning of sorrow. Even all the care and thought of those at home will be little to meet the suffering.

Love for the soldiers is hysterical. At the railway stations where the wounded arrive wait large crowds of women with baskets of gifts ; and when the huge cross-marked, comfortable ambulance train comes in and stops, there is a new and sweet invasion—all the girls running along the corridors with cigarettes, with tea and sugar, and cakes and newspapers.

Even on wet evenings the dense, uncomplaining crowd waits for the wounded and the prisoners, and, as the great red cross of the slowly approaching ambulance train looms through the darkness you may hear sad whispered exclamations among the crowd—"*Lord ! Lord !* "

Even the German wounded participate in the general hospitality, and you frequently hear a Russian woman say of the wounded enemy before her, "Poor one; is it his fault that he is fighting us?" The Germans, for their part, are very suspicious, asking of the tea, "Is it not vitriol?" refusing to take medicine, and asking "When are we to be hanged?"

The streets of the city present many sights—the marching of soldiers, the endless stream of the army moving out of the depths of Russia to the war; a magnificent peasantry, brought in some cases from the remotest places of the Old World. They sing as they march, they lift their hats and shout as they go, cheering for the war. In the midst of their number are many peasant women, wives who refuse to be parted from their husbands, and they help to carry the immense baggage.

As a contrast, there are long processions of German and Austrian prisoners, looking very sulky and tired; men in battered helmets, rent clothes, cavalrymen without horses, foot-soldiers with the dust and blood of the battlefield unremoved. Russians guard them with drawn swords on their shoulders, the populace runs alongside and laughs and criticises: "What small men! William promised they should come to Moscow, and they've come!"

No malice, however, seems to be borne the prisoners. On the contrary, they are shown a great deal of kindness. Sausage is provided for them and German newspapers. Many people ask, "Is it not dull for you here?" "Not so dull if only there were beer," is the reply.

Or, as upon the festival of Dmitri Donskoi, there come men with horns, men with bells and with gongs, making a great din, and criers shouting, and pantechnicon vans attended by society ladies, merchants' wives, and pretty actresses. Into these vans you throw what-. ever you fancy, promiscuously. Bright girls come into your lodgings, and you give them all the old clothes you don't want, or the new warm things you have prepared for the occasion, and they take them and throw them into the vans; people just coming out of shops with parcels in their hands throw the parcels into the vans on the impulse. The vans go to the richest and to the poorest streets. From the poorest they take even rags and tatters; all can be put to use in the service of the soldiers, who, perchance, have to go through a cold winter in the trenches.

There are frequent hurrahs on the streets as motor-cars tear past with wounded men being taken to the hospitals. Outside all the places to which for the time being wounded are being carried there are crowds waiting. When the cars stop at the hospital door there is a chorus of cheers and exclamations: *Bravo! Molotsi!* (fine fellows). *Spasebo!* (thanks); and the soldiers answer, "Cheer up, we're winning!"

I visit Pereplotchikof and find him looking much older, as if the autumn of life had breathed over the summer of his prime. But he is very active, and has a dozen war notebooks in his pocket. He spent the summer quietly in a village on the Northern Dwina, and when the war broke out returned directly to Moscow. He saw the Tsar, as also did my Liavlia friend Alexey Sergeitch,* now a Liberal tutor in a prince's house. The unguarded Tsar was as free and cheerful in Moscow as if he had never heard of revolutions, nihilists, assassins.

With the outbreak of the war, literature and art came

---

* One of the revolutionaries mentioned in "Undiscovered Russia." Varvara Sergevna, his sister, is now a Red Cross nurse.

to an end. "I am no longer a painter," says Pereplotchikof. "I have almost forgotten that I used to paint
pictures." Pereplotchikof serves on six committees for
the care of the wounded. Maxim Gorky has volunteered
to go to the front with the Red Cross. The author of
"Jealousy" and "Sanin" works at the Brest Station
all day like a porter, carrying wounded soldiers from
the just-arrived Red Cross trains to the ambulances and
motor-cars and Red Cross trams waiting to convey them
to the hospitals. Nothing is now more familiar than the
double-coach Red Cross tramcars gliding slowly along
the iron ways, full of wounded, the first coach with plain
glass, full of those lightly injured, the second with ground
glass, but open windows, showing a dozen or twenty
upper and lower beds laden with the heavily wounded.

All the doss-houses, and many schools and churches,
are occupied by the wounded. People of all ranks in
society are working together for their care. As I sit
with Pereplotchikof, the telephone bell rings. It is to
say that a certain big doss-house is much in need of
Bibles and books of a religious character, a few gramophones are asked for; and some women might help,
reading aloud, writing letters, and chatting to the
illiterate. The nurses have all their spare time occupied
in writing love-letters to the soldiers' sweethearts.

I accompanied my friend to the doss-house, an
immense building near the Riazansky Station. The
chief doctor showed me round. I expected to see a
very mournful spectacle, but was agreeably surprised.
Not one in twenty of the wounded was lying in his
bed. Every hall was full of gaiety and life; the soldiers
walking about in their white undergarments, talking,
reading, laughing, playing cards; men with bandaged

Vodka and the Doss-house

legs, bandaged hands, heads, bodies, with their bare feet stuck into hospital slippers.

The doctor, who confessed to a great admiration for the English, took me into the operating room, a place of blood and disinfectant; into the bandaging room, where a young soldier was having his arm tied up anew; into the big basement hall, where the daily cabbage soup is served out.

"What has happened to the tramps and beggars who used to sleep here o' nights?" I asked.

"There are fewer of them," said the doctor. "Since the sale of vodka stopped and the war began, the old night population seems to have vanished. I do not know how much good the war will ultimately bring, but the sobriety which it has already brought would justify it."

The wounded are full of their impressions of the war and of Germany, and they talk readily. Thus: "Germany is a fine country, no comparison with our poor villages—stone houses, brick houses, three storeys, fine carpets, chairs, gramophones. Every house has a gramophone, and we all learned how to set them going. One day, I had just come into a house and set a gramophone going, when an officer puts his head into the broken window and says, 'Stop that music at once!' I didn't know how to stop it, so I just hits it, *biff*, in the middle of the wheel and it goes into bits all over the room. Then they have fiddles, and every house has a big black box with a lid (piano), and when you open the lid and bang it with your hand it goes '*bir, bir, bir; bo, bo, bo.*'"

"Is there plenty to eat?" "Yes, pigs, as many as you like. We had roast German pork every day;

hundreds, thousands of pigs. We caught them, and carried them to the camp." The wounded man hunts in the sack by his bedside and brings out a murderous looking knife. "That's what the Germans kill them with," he says.

Many wounded have trophies taken from the dead and from the houses of the ransacked villages—watches, rings, guns; one we saw had a bracelet. A wounded officer whom we met at another place told us how the streets of the German towns were strewn with books, gramophones, vases, silver-plate, white piano keys in handfuls, but no pictures, no statues. The soldiers never touch any pictures, not even that of the Emperor William—saying merely of him as they look at his picture on the wall: "How the ends of his moustache are turned up!" "We'll turn them down for him, eh, brothers?" The wounded are always asked—"Do the Germans fight well?" and they answer, "Yes, like dogs"; or "Not with the bayonet. They carry their bayonets in their belts; we always have ours fixed and ready. They are afraid of the hand-to-hand struggle. They think the Cossacks are devils who live far away in the forests like savages, living on raw meat and blood. They are all afraid of the Cossacks."

There is great enthusiasm wherever people are gathered together, and you know that all the talk is war—war only. It is difficult to get seated at a restaurant and make a meal, owing to the number of times national anthems are called for. Every minute or so an officer comes in, orders a bottle of wine, and then, taking glass in hand, stands up and says, "Gentlemen, our adored monarch!" or, "Gentlemen, our noble allies.—Vive la France!"; or, "Gentlemen, the Eng-

A Cossack's Exploit

lish!"—"The Belgians!" and the orchestra goes through the national hymns while the toasts are drunk.

One of the wounded who appeared at Moscow was Kuzma Krutchkof, the first to receive the ribbon of the Order of St. George for bravery. He gave a fine account of himself. He is a handsome young man, dark, slender, with a clever look on his sunburnt face.

"It was like this," he said. "On the 30th of July,* at ten o'clock in the morning, we set out from the town of Calvary to Alexandrovo. There were four of us—I and my friends Ivan Schtegolkof, Vassily Astakhof, and Michael Ivanof. As we were climbing a little hill we came up against a detachment of German soldiers from the 9th Lancers, twenty-seven men with two officers. At first the Germans were afraid, but afterwards they made a dash at us. They had the advantage of position, because they were on the hill and we below them. However, we stood to them steadily and killed a few of them as they came. In evading their attack we got separated from one another—Schtegolkof fought on my left; on my right, near a bit of marsh, fought Astakhof and Ivanof. There were eleven Germans fighting me. I did not expect to remain alive, but I resolved to sell my life dearly. My horse was agile and obedient. I wanted to use my rifle, but in my haste the cartridge slipped out. A German slashed at my fingers, so I threw the rifle down, seized my sword and sat to work. I got several slight wounds, and I felt the blood flowing from them, but I knew they were not serious. For every wound I got I gave back a deadly blow which quieted a German for ever. An officer sprang at me, but I repulsed his attack and made him run and then chased him. When I caught

* Russian time.

27

him up, I waved my sword and hacked at his head, but only dented his helmet. I struck out again, but the officer jerked his head aside as he dashed along, and my sword caught him on the neck and almost completely cut his head off. I killed a few more men, but I began to feel that my sword was difficult to wield, so I caught hold of one of the German lances and killed all the others in turn with it.

"Meanwhile my friends had managed the rest of them very cleverly. Twenty-four corpses lay on the ground, some being dragged about in terror by the horses. My friends were a little hurt and I had sixteen wounds, but they were all 'nothing,' just cuts on the back, on my neck, and on my hands. My horse was hurt in eleven places, too, but he carried me back for six versts without being attended to. Then he got weaker, and a peasant carried us the other four versts in his cart. After our wounds had been bound up, they sent the four of us to the hospital, and afterwards here to Moscow, though I asked to stay in Vitevsk, because there was no need for me to go to Moscow—it only meant troubling the authorities, and we were quite well. On the 14th of August, General Rennenkampf came to me, and, taking off his Order of St. George, pinned it on my breast, and congratulated me on receiving it.

"My horse is alive and well. To-morrow I am off again to the war—it is dull for a healthy fellow to be here doing nothing. After our fight with the Germans, only our boots and caps were whole. All the rest of our clothes were cut and torn to bits. However, the fight was not much—the Germans cannot use their lances well; they hold them stupidly under their arms, and cannot wield them about; you can easily beat them off

Songs of the Russian Soldiers

and hurt them, especially on our good horses. I am married—yes; all of us are married. I have two young sons, healthy little fellows. I'll see them again some day, if God wills. But our Cossack women and children must get used to accidents."

Kuzma has his picture in all the newspapers, but he has now returned to the war.

Moscow is full of stories, for the convalescent are up and about, and three times, seven times, kill the slain. At the bath-houses of the city, it is amusing to see naked soldiers exhibiting their wounds and telling the stories of their battles to an admiring throng of civilians, amusing to see the siege of garrulous soldiers in the streets, in the taverns (where only tea is sold), and in the tramcars. Moscow is very near to the war.

I met, at the house of Vassily Vassilitch, a young officer just returned from the front with dispatches, and he gave a very interesting account of the state of the conquered territory in Eastern Prussia. He is a cousin of one of my Moscow friends, a tall, energetic young man with sunburnt face, eyes wide-opened, as in astonishment, eyes that you feel have *seen things*, lips parted as if startled, voice still hoarse from shouting commands upon the battlefield.

"Well, what is it all like out there?"

He takes a chair, puts it back facing you, and sits astride of it, and begins to talk as if bursting with the need to tell his story.

"How do we fight? Oh, splendid! The forward movement is accomplished singing. The Germans seem distressed by the songs of the Russians as they fight. Yes, the Germans are just as brave as we are. They stick to it to the last point. When captured, they behave very correctly, and to all questions answer, 'I have no information to give.' They will answer no questions whatever."

"How do the German population behave?"

"*Nevazhno;* not very well. They shoot at us. They spy a great deal, and have been able to give much information by means of the subterranean telephone. We could not understand how it was the German artillery fire was so skilfully directed, till we discovered the underground telephone. In a basement cellar one day we actually found an eighty-five-year-old crone telephoning to the enemy. During our questioning she had a fit and died of fright."

"What are the towns like—Insterburg, for instance?"

"Insterburg is a fine town, about the size of Nizhni-Novgorod. Life isn't much upset. Business goes on. The value of a rouble has been fixed at three marks, and everything is cheap. We sometimes fear poison, and there have been some cases of poisoning, but the inhabitants are afraid of punishment. As for shooting from windows, we have fixed a tariff—first shot from a house, we blow up the house; second shot from the same street, we blow up the street. That is grim earnest on our part. Gumbinen is a smaller town, and is in rather a bad state. Eydkunen is a terrible sight, has no semblance of a town. When I came through with my regiment, the only thing we found was beer; the cellars were full of it. Our men, who had not had beer or vodka for a month, went mad over it. There was a stream of beer down the main street. You must understand there was not a soul there but ourselves, not a house that was not blackened by fire, not a window that was not broken, not a room that had not been ransacked. Precious things of all kinds lay in the streets, ruined and soaked by rain.

Impression of East Prussia

"As for the villages, they have mostly been looted or burned. The Germans fire them as they retire. Often at night we have been glad of the light of the burning farms and villages, helping to find our wounded on the battlefield. The conflagrations made night like day.

"Yes; it makes a melancholy impression to go through village after village, blackened, deserted, looted. Once I noticed a ripe apple on a tree in one of the looted villages; it caused me some surprise. It was something that had escaped the plunderer.

"It is dangerous travelling alone or in twos. Even this conquered country is full of ambushes. The people are extremely hostile. There are robber bands, detachments of German cavalry as yet uncaptured, armed bicyclists. Many soldiers skulk in the woods. It is good for us that the German roads are so firm, and we can make journeys much more quickly than in the sand or mud of Russian Poland."

"What is going to happen next up there?"

"Oh, a big battle, most likely. The Germans are straining every nerve to arrange a big defeat for us. Every one who can hold a gun is being pressed into service against us. We know that by the dead they leave in the field; men without uniforms and in their usual civilian attire, many sailors from their warships, children of fifteen and sixteen, old men past the age of fighting. Progress is very difficult, but the news of the success in Austria inspires us, as no doubt it 'dispirits the enemy. And, as every one knows, we have an ,enormous number of men in the background—fresh, eager. I go back, myself, with reinforcements."

"How did you feel under fire?"

"It was unpleasant at first, but after awhile it became

even pleasant, exhilarating. One feels an extraordinary freedom in the midst of death, with bullets whistling round. The same with all the soldiers: the wounded all want to get well and return to the fight. They fight with tears of joy in their eyes."

"They feel active hate towards the Germans?"

"No; I wouldn't say that. They regard them merely as the enemy—the old enemy."

"There is a certain beauty in going to death with songs," said I.

"I would even say there is no greater beauty," says the young officer.

So war comes into its own in the popular imagination. Despite the praise of peace and the comfort of peace, and even the fact that we are fighting to obtain peace, war seems to be a thing that must eternally recur—one of the human liturgies of beauty.

WHY RUSSIA IS FIGHTING

BRITAIN is fighting for disarmament and universal peace. France is fighting to save herself from the monster who has already devoured a portion of her side, Alsace and Lorraine. Germany is fighting to impose her order on the rest of the world, to make us all, as it were, don German uniforms. Germany has had great dreams; one of them was of a German and Austrian belt from Heligoland to Constantinople; another was of a finally subjugated France and possibly of a Belgium absorbed into the German Empire. Germany, taking herself seriously as the standard-bearer of Western civilisation, considers that she has carried order, cleanliness, education and national efficiency to a point of perfection unattainable by the people of other countries. Russia is fighting to preserve her national life and religion.

Of all nations the most abhorrent to the Germans must be the Russians. The Russian character, temperament and mind are all opposed to the German soul. The Russian subtlety and contradictoriness, the Russian mysticism and unpracticality, above all things Russian national untidiness, are intolerable to the German. The German is filled with loathing directly he passes the Russian frontier; the difference between the well-built towns, storehouses, and firm highways of Eastern Prussia and the wildernesses of Russian Poland is almost incredible. To enter Russia is to step down into an inferior world, a world that needs setting right.

Russia and the World

" Russia offers wonderful material for the making of history," said Bismarck; "let but its feminine type of population be interbred with our strong, masculine Germans." " The Slavonic peoples are not a nation," wrote the Emperor William, "but rather soil on which a nation with a historic mission might be grown."

In this it is impossible not to see a considerable amount of German stupidity. The Germans are going to suffer terribly through their ignorance of the strength of Russia, through their inability to realise to what an extent the Russians are national. It is because of their national individuality and of their vast population of like faith, like tongue, and like point of view that the Russians go to the front in confidence. When the Germans attack the Russians they are attacking a nation that has a background of 8,000 miles.

The war has come as a relief to Russia, uniting all parties under one idea. For a long while Russia has been subjected to a strong German influence. Germany has long felt that "something might be done" with Russia, and it has done all it could to give a Germanising tint to Russian government. It is not without significance, that story in Dostoieffsky's "Adult," of the German who shot himself through vexation at the idea that Russia might come to nothing. The brutality with which the Russian revolutionary movement was put down was not only approved by the Germans, but received a considerable amount of inspiration from them.

Prince Trubetskoy in a recent article is even ready to say that there lies a German hidden under many Russian breasts. If that is so, it may account for many

Getting Rid of the German Spirit in Life

a brutal act and much of the feeling of oppression in Russia. When war was declared Russia suddenly grew lighter, as if an evil spirit had jumped off her back. German subjects were put under arrest and sent to remote places. German shops were closed; German goods tabooed. Berlinskaya Street became Londonskaya, Petersburg became Petrograd, Schlusselburg became Oreshof, Kronstadt something else; in many schools the German language was given up and English taken instead; the Hotel Vienna three doors from me became the Hotel of Holy Victory. But not only that. A little German devil of harshness and iron-heeledness jumped out and disappeared, and the Grand Duke Commander-in-Chief proclaimed reconciliation to the Poles, and every one became kinder to one another. People in Russia are naturally kind; they have become even gentler since the war began.

"The German title *Graf* is related to the Russian verb *grabit*, to grab, to steal," says Rozanof, of the *Novoe Vremya*. "The Germans have always been a predatory race as far as the Slavs are concerned. They are the very opposite of the Russians. In the whole of Russian literature there is not one page in which mockery is made of poverty, of suffering, of a girl who has been betrayed, or of a child that is illegitimate. Russian literature is one long hymn to the injured and insulted." *

The whole of Russian popular feeling is of tenderness rather than rapacity, and though, of course, there lurks in the Russian soul not only the brutal German but the more brutal Tartar, yet it is love to one another, fellow-sympathy in suffering, and gentle sociability that keep the great nation together. It is these that unite

* V. V. Rozanof, "The Russian Idea."

35

them round the sacred ark of the race. The Germans, sneering at the weak and at the victims of their lust for power, with their brutal materialism and their cruelty, represent that which is most foreign to the Russian heart, and consequently that which is most abhorred by all the people.

One of the commonest headings in Russian papers is "Holy War." A war, if it is going to have any success in Russia, must be a holy war. The Crimean War was a holy war to protect the Russian pilgrims from the persecutions of the Turks. The Japanese War never succeeded in getting thought holy—that was why it failed so disastrously. This war is holy to every one, and its motto is—getting rid of the German spirit in life, getting rid of the sheer materialistic point of view, getting rid of brutality and the lack of understanding of others. The great spiritual power of the war has worked miracles in the social life of the people.

How seriously the war is taken! "What do you make of the war?" I asked a well-known Russian the other day.

"It is the Last Judgment," said he. "Every one has been handed in his account. Now we've got to get square with Destiny. We must realise all our resources of will, and faith, and health, and put them in front of our national life to save it. It reminds me of the crisis in the drama of 'Peer Gynt.' You remember when the button-moulder came and said to Peer that his day was done, and that he must be put into the melting-pot and recast as someone else. Peer searched in his history and in his life to get something that could redeem him. Only in the peasant girl Solveig did he find refuge from the moulder. So with Russia—to her also the button-

Russia and the Melting-Pot

moulder has come and offered to melt her up with a strong alloy of Germany into something new. She must go to her peasants if she wishes to remain herself. In the hour of distress it is our peasants who will save us."

Russia, above all things, is fighting that she may go on being herself. Every one who loves Russia believes in her personal destiny. She is the youngest of the nations ; she has a great life before her.

We fight, and the year grows colder and more bitter. The yellow leaves are falling day by day, and winter is at hand. Commissaries are in Moscow buying heavy overcoats for the Army for winter, and we know that the war becomes heavier, gloomier. Yet now and again we spare a glance beyond winter and ask, what will it be like when the foe is beaten?

Will not Russia emerge greater than before — the true mother of the Slav races ? Will not the Eastern Church remain unshaken, surer of itself, with all its heritage of early Christian tradition and present-day spiritual strength ?

IS IT A LAST WAR?

ALL the same, I do not believe in this war as a last war, or in this war as "a war of things," a war of ammunition, rifles, and clothes, rather than of men and ideals and emotions, a war that is only a matter of mathematics or addition and subtraction.

I have just read in Russian translation an article by H. G. Wells on this war as a war of things, a war of equipment and machines. "Things also make war," says the Russian translation. And the Editor of the Russian paper insists on the lessons of that remarkable western book, "A World Set Free," and on the power of material things to put the world right. We British, alas, are only too ready to think that it is *things* that count. It gives rest to our souls to fix the responsibility upon something solid and material and accepted. Hence our passion for things, Acts of Parliament, book regulations, equipments, conventions.

What we really need is a younger generation that has faith in England's destiny, we need a nation physically fit, we need knowledge and training so that we do not in future wait until the time of war to learn what are, for instance, the possibilities of the use of submarines and of floating mines. We need brains used for the nation's sake. And last of all, as Mr. Wells says, "we do, of course, need manufacture."

As a matter of fact we have got manufacture, we don't need to ask for it. "I can't get out of the

Russia Wins in spite of Bad Equipment

habit of thinking in dozens of gross," said a London manufacturer to me the other day.

We go on manufacturing like the quern at the bottom of the sea. There was once a wonderful quern which came into the possession of a stupid man, and he said to it, "Grind me herrings and soup, and grind them quickly and well." Unfortunately, he did not know how to stop the machine, and it is grinding out herrings and soup to this day. Hence the Atlantic Ocean.

The German schoolmaster is our foe more than the German manufacturer. The longer time German children stay at school, and the bigger sacrifice of time given to military training, tell tremendously in this national struggle. As William Watson writes in one of his poems

> " It's ignorance, ignorance, ignorance
> Will pull Old England down."

Yes, ignorance, lack of national faith, lack of good bodies. Only England will not be pulled down; we do not intend to let her.

It has been averred that Russia was prepared for war, having the things ready. But that is to make a great mistake. The Russians are winning their battles because of their religious faith, their physical strength, and their sobriety. Not because of their *things*, their equipment. It is the Russians' bare breast in the mouth of the cannon, their songs against the roar of artillery. They are inferior in guns, inferior in aircraft, inferior in the quality of their boots. They have frozen and starved as no Germans could freeze or starve. And they have won. The panoply of Goliath is very sug-

39

gestive. It wins battles for the Philistines. But let us
not insist on it ; it is the other side of the question
that we as a nation are most ready to forget.

I read constantly in the Russian papers our English
and French opinions that this war is a last war, a war
for disarmament and universal peace, a final effort to
crush "barbarism." The socialists are to depose the
Kaiser. The working men of England are to enter into
alliance with the working men of foreign countries to
avert war in the future. The working men in Russia
and the liberal bourgeoisie are greatly edified by this.
They find in it another instance of the greatness of
England. England, as ever, leads the other nations, and
shows them the ideal. She moves step by step towards
the millennium.

But despite the pleasing sentiment, is it not probable
that as a result of the war militarism will increase
throughout the whole world ? We shall probably beat
Germany, but we shall probably arrange with her a
generous peace—not a humiliating peace. Russia will
remain a great military nation, the foundation of whose
aristocracy is military rank, and not, as with us in England, civil title. Mighty Japan will remain. Italy, who
wantonly acquired Tripoli, will remain. England, with
her Dreadnoughts and with perhaps the navy taken from
the Germans, and possibly with some system of conscription, will remain. And war has become more
interesting.

There is one nation that sincerely wishes peace, and
that is America. It is fortunate for America that her
people speak English and seem to be English by race
We British give them a sentimental protection, and also
as it happens, an accidental protection. If Germany

The Afrai Village-church.

The Great Symphony of the War

won, America would be in danger. As it is, the extreme wealth of the American people sheds a baleful light on her destiny. As war goes on, with its tremendous expense, America gains financial preponderance day by day. She will be in a position to hold Europe in bondage when the war is over. She seems destined to attract to herself more and more European hate.

The world in which the armies move up and down and against one another, in which there have been in the past cultures greater than our own, where, since everlasting, wise men have risen and spoken, poets sung, priests anointed to sacrifice—is the hurly-burly, which remains ever the same. It is a mystery play planned by the gods, and we all know our parts involuntarily. But it is not a play in five acts, it goes on for ever. It does not give an intellectual satisfaction, but a sensuous pleasure. The whispering of the nations together, the conspiracy, the march of men, the clash of arms, the flow of blood, the dance of death—it blends in idea and streams up to heaven in a great symphony.

AUTUMN LEAVES

WHEN I went to see Vassily Vassilitch one day he said to me, "Have you heard the earth crying?"

"What do you mean?" I asked.

"Why," said he, "I've heard her crying. As I lay in the grass with my ear to the ground I heard her. Like this—*oo-m, oo-m, oo-m*. It was the time the soldiers were being mobilised and women were sobbing in every cottage and at every turning of the road, so it may only have been that I heard. But it seemed to me the earth herself was crying, so gently, so sadly, that my own heart ached."

I understood what he meant. One night in September when I saw the first big, moist, yellow leaves come down on the wind, a thought whispered itself to my heart— the soldiers are dying. As I lay abed, long after midnight, and listened to the moaning wind I thought what many will think this autumn—the leaves are falling, falling—and away, far away on the battlefield, the soldiers are dying, dying. Listen to the wind in the trees, and you hear the great storm wind of Odin roaring through the Life-tree Yggdrasil. You hear the rush of the Valkyries, the Choosers of the slain.

All the way from Moscow to the seat of war the forests are yellow and red, and the glades and meadows are strewn with dead leaves. Only on the fringe of the Baltic is it green as in England at this time of the year.

Nearer to the War

But even on the Baltic shore the symbol is showing. Such a violent gale is raging that leaves and stems are broken off before their time, and the feet tread gently on a moving carpet of wrenched leaves.

In Moscow on the boulevards hundreds of little children with spades and pails make sand castles and fortifications and play at war whilst the leaves dance round them in circles and spirals. At Libau on the seashore the leaves race past mingled in clouds of blinding sand, whilst beside them, and, as it were, attacking them, the great black turbulent sea turns over white in a dozen lines of foaming waves and thundering rollers. The white steeds of the sea rush up and spend themselves and die as if they also were in the great war.

Good, however, to be nearer the war, to be, as it were, on the way to the war, and going with the soldiers. When the war broke out there was a strange strain on the mind. The feeling in London and Paris, in England and France, was no doubt sharper, more terrible; but even far away in the depths of Russia, where there was little news and where the fighting seemed remotest of all, there was a strain. We were tired out at the end of the day even though we had been doing nothing. Questions for which there were no answers incessantly dinned at the brain—

"What does it mean?" "What will be the end of it?" "Is England safe?" All night long objurgatory thrills passed through the body as if one were a sort of psychic seismometer. Moscow nights were nights of bad dreams wherein one suddenly became awake and exclaimed under the breath such things as, "This brings an era to a close." "When this is over we may as well start again numbering from the year One."

43

Russia and the World

It was a great relief when I felt free to leave Moscow and could set out for the front. It was as if the mind were a bird tired with vain flight over boundless seas, and the bird had seen an island whereon to come to rest.

I arrived at Libau at eight o'clock. All was dark. There was not a street lamp. The gas was turned low in the railway station and the blinds were drawn. The blinds were drawn in every house, and only by chinks of light could you tell that the city was not abandoned. As I sat in a cab going to an hotel a tramcar came slowly past with dim lights showing many people. Even the lights of the car had been shrouded in little curtains. There were no people on the pavements and only my cab in the street. We crossed a bridge and saw the masts and black funnels of many ships—but never a light among them. The lamp was not lit on the lighthouse. The pier was black. The cinema theatre was closed and empty.

I went into the hotel, once the Petersburg, now the Petrograd Hotel, and obtained a room. The Swiss spoke to me in German, the attendant showing me my room spoke German, the waiter addressed me in German. It seemed to me they might as well have left the name standing as Petersburg.

The population of all the district along the Baltic shore takes its stand rather as German than as Russian. Riga, Windau, Mittau, Libau, and many other towns are more German than Russian. The High Street, the *glavnaya ulitsa* as it is in Russian, is in these towns the Grosse Strasse. The tramcar stops at the Halt Platz. The newspapers sold are all *Zeitungs* and *Tageblatts*. The children talk German in the streets, the Jews talk German in the markets. Even Russian officers and Sisters of Mercy are heard talking German together. It is, therefore, rather in vain that the Government, as I read to-day, is going to re-name all the streets and suburbs and institutions by Russian names. Let what is German so remain !

A cautious population that of Libau ! Four-fifths of the business people are German Jews, and they have considerable hope that they will not suffer too much if the Germans should come in. Nevertheless, they have sent their women and their valuables into the depths of the country. I am told that after the shelling of Libau, in the first flush of the idea that the Germans were coming in, many tradesmen refused to speak or understand Russian. Whether these false citizens had some understanding with the Germans seems to be a matter for investigation.

Libau was never in flames. That was the first lie of the war. It was shelled and one shell fell on the sand, but all the others fell into the sea. No one was hurt, no damage done. The German fleet has not reappeared.

The city is under martial law; no lights are allowed at night, all visitors to the town have to show their passports at once, sentries march up and down the seashore, there is a military patrol of the streets. It is generally felt that if it is Germany's intention to wage at any time an active and not merely a passive war with Russia, this territory, so German in its sympathies, is most liable to invasion. It can be invaded either by land or by sea. In any case, until the German fleet is destroyed or greatly weakened the Baltic ports will fear attack.

That is why I came up to Libau. I should not

Russia and the World

be surprised at any moment to hear the sound of guns. Every day there are crowds of people on the sands staring out to sea, as if they were likely to see ships of war. But necessarily I shall not wait. I go on southward along the line of the struggle—as near as the authorities will let me go.

A strange impression of Libau I take away with me —the empty and far-raging sea outside the town, and the quiet harbour inside it. The harbour is a strange sight with all the ships standing motionless and empty, the big black and red British ship, *Bannockburn;* the bulky *Baltica,* of the Baltic Lloyd Company; a ship for some reason or trick painted with a huge red cross; the *Vorms,* the *Folsjo,* the *Commerce,* the *Aira,* the *Kazan;* passenger ships plying to London, others to New York. This Libau is the chief port from which sail ordinarily the emigrants, the 300,000 Jews, Russians, Poles, and Lithuanians who leave Russia annually for America, but who are now closed in their Motherland against their custom. The warehouses are all padlocked, the quays are bare and empty, no dockers, no watchmen. Not a man on all these vessels, not a puff of steam from a funnel or a pipe in them. All is quiet and empty.

THE ECONOMIC ISOLATION OF RUSSIA

RUSSIA at the beginning of the war expected to be shut within herself and cut off from the rest of Europe, it seems. Libau and Riga and the rest of the Baltic ports were dead, so far as shipping is concerned. The Black Sea was stoppered at the Bosphorus, and the ports of Odessa, Sebastopol, Novorossisk, and Batum were consequently rendered idle. The Arctic Ocean was considerably enlivened as a result of the war; Archangel has become a great port, receiving American liners, passenger steamers from England, and cargo boats in great numbers. English steamers have sailed down the River Ob as far as Tomsk—but the Arctic closes early. Towards the end of October the port of Archangel freezes, and cannot be kept open later than Christmas, even with the help of ice-breakers. European traffic with Russia ceases, except by the Gulf of Bothnia and Sweden. But mines have been laid along the Finnish coast of the Gulf of Bothnia, and Russian trade seems likely to flow through Vladivostok alone for a while.*

The results of the blockade are noticeable in Russia. Ordinarily Russia exports an enormous quantity of foodstuffs—grain, butter, sugar eggs, meat, and so on—and as a consequence of her inability to discharge these products she has an immense superabundance of them on her hands. Directly the war began it was possible to note in Siberia what may be called "the returning tide of

* The railroad and motor-car service from Bergen, in Norway, to Petrograd, via the North of Sweden and Torneó, remains open (February, 1915).

butter "; butter had no exit and would not keep, and
therefore had to be sold to people at home at any price
—the peasant women in Siberia began to use butter for
themselves since it was so cheap. There has been
a general cheapening of food, and not only has the cost
of living not increased as a result of the war, but it has
decreased. But the value of the Russian rouble has gone
down twenty-two per cent. owing to Russia's inability to
export her products.*

And though food has remained cheap other things
have become dear. The import of manufactured goods
into Russia has almost ceased. Germany used to export
to Russia immense quantities of utensils and chemically
prepared materials. Nearly all the medicines came from
Germany, and there is now a great famine in drugs.
Even for the wounded and the sick there is a scarcity
of medicine, and it costs a great deal more than it
should do to cure the poor soldier. Ink costs more
than it did; photographic materials, clothes, Vienna
boots cost fifty per cent. more; Paris hats and costumes
are disappearing. Russian women are going to be without
fashions for a long time to come.

So the middle and upper classes will feel the pinch
of the war; but the poor, who do not ask for anything
more than food, will be better off, especially as they
are saved the great former waste of money on vodka
and beer. There are no unemployed, the beggars have
almost all disappeared. Women and children are working in the factories on day and night shifts. Money is
flowing like water, and, for all manner of reasons, life

* On July 30th the exchange was 95, now it is 116. This means that it costs
the Russian Government £22 more on every £100 of interest they pay on foreign
debt, that the Russian merchant who pays in sterling has to pay 22 per cent. more
for what he imports.

The Loss of Labouring Hands

is brisk. War is a great spending of savings. The great rush of military expense has floated many a poverty-stricken family and given it money and interest and life.

The vigour of the Russian Government at once became evident, and was well exemplified by the action as regards vodka and beer. In no other country in the world could drinking be stopped, as it were, by a stroke of the Monarch's pen. It has always been said that vodka afforded so much revenue that the Tsar would never take really active steps to suppress it. But, here, in the midst of the greatest financial need, he sacrificed an enormous revenue in order to save and strengthen his people in the time of danger. To-day the shutters are up in every Government monopoly shop of the vast Russian Empire. It is a stupendous fact.

It is sad to see so many wounded soldiers who have lost two or three fingers. It seems trifling compared with body wounds, but in reality the loss of fingers is more pitiful. It means an end to useful toil, an end also to shouldering the rifle for the Motherland. That is what war means economically; the loss of labouring hands in the building of the State. Russia was taken in the midst of things by this war. How many railways she was constructing, how many towns she was building!

All lies idle now as I write, and the autumn rains drench down on thousands of scaffoldings and melancholy heaps of bricks and mortar, left as they were on the day of mobilisation. It is interesting to speculate how the contracts are being fulfilled on the Central Asian Railway and on the Altai Railway. Many prisoners of war are being drafted on to the work. A number of these unfortunate Teutons will taste the sorrows of a Siberian winter.* They must take the place of those who are fighting.

It is astonishing to think of it. Practically all the able-bodied men of the immense tract of Russia and Siberia are now on the German and Austrian frontier. Their customary work all remains behind ! They have not a thought for it. Their eyes look ever forward to Berlin and Vienna. Here at Koshedari, where I write, thirty miles from the Nieman, I watch the fresh troops still coming in every day from Russia. The trains do not suffice to take them, they go forward on foot, on horseback, in wagons and carts, with food supplies, with saddles, with fodder, with officers, baggage and equipments. They are all in clean and unfrayed uniforms, the faces are fresh and simple ; a contrast to those who return from the front, all dust and mud, their faces set, their eyes glaring. What confidence there is among the soldiers ! Youngsters with faint down on their lips and cheeks come prancing past on their horses, holding their black Cossack lances with the assurance of men who have spent all their lives fighting. Their officers look much more resourceful and able than ever they did in peace. The war has made them.

They all go forward to death or victory. The river of Time has reached the rapids, and the smooth current of existence has reached Niagara. Boys have become men ; young men middle-aged men ; middle-aged men old men. They all fly to destiny.

*By February, 1915, there were over 200,000 Austrian and German prisoners in Siberia. Even far-away Yakutsk, with a winter where 60° of frost is nothing unusual, has its hundred or so. There are several thousands at Irkutsk, at Barnaul, at Kranoyarsk, at Tashkent. They have the hardest time of all prisoners, since the Russian standard of living is so low and the rigour of the climate so unexampled. It is reported that many Germans have expressed their gladness to be captured and so out of the struggle. But if so they did not know what was in store for them—the task of replacing industrially those who have been taken from Siberia to fight.

ON THE RIVER NIEMAN

GRODNO, on the River Nieman, is one of those miserable towns of the Jewish Pale, crowded with a poverty-stricken and slatternly humanity. Panic has ranged there ever since the German invasion. First it was crowded with penniless refugees from Suvalki and the country round about, and then, in its turn, its own people began to flee. Nearly all the women and children left the town. The streets are crowded with Russian soldiers, who outnumber the rest of the population by twenty to one. The shops are sold out of half their merchandise, for the soldiers buy up everything edible. One passenger train a day leaves for Vilna and one for Warsaw, and they are packed with refugees. Six or seven trains of soldiers leave every day to reinforce the troops at Lodz and Petrokof. Trains of wounded arrive ; horse and motor wagons of them arrive by the road.

I saw many soldiers' funeral services held in the little wooden churches put up in the hospital yards. Here lay the dead warriors in their open coffins, with crowns on their heads, their faces like marble. Scores of soldiers, chance passers-by, held candles and stood round the dead ones and crossed themselves and kissed the marble faces a last good-bye. "How did this one die ? How did this one die ? " I heard in whispers. "Shrapnel, shrapnel," came the whispered answer. The coffins were lifted by the soldiers, a dozen for each coffin, and hoisted on the

shoulders—the wood that held the dead lay against
the cheeks of the living as the procession went out
through the town, with standards and standard-bearers,
and priests in their vestments. Many of the soldiers
taking part in the service were those who had not
yet been under fire, but who were going forward that
very night. The idea of how soon they might be white
and dead, like those they carried, must have crossed
their minds; but death calms a Russian, it does not
unnerve him. The soldiers' faces were calm and
steadfast.

This was a Sunday afternoon; all day, all evening, all
night it rained. I spent many hours at the railway
station watching the trains go off; watching German
prisoners being brought in; talking to the wounded,
and being myself cross-questioned by a police agent,
who thought me a suspicious character. About ten
o'clock I walked through the town to see what might
be going on. There in the ghetto I saw a touching
sight. A score of carts had come in from the country
and the battlefield, not the ordinary carts with tilts, but
those long, narrow contrivances on which the peasant
timber men brought from the forest to the sawmill
whole pine logs—twenty of these on loose and blunder-
ing wheels were clattering over the cobbles and bumps
and holes of a poor street. In them lay wounded
soldiers wrapped in brown blankets, just as they had
been picked up from the field of victory. Every twenty
paces the carts stopped in order that the wounded
might rest from the terrible jolting, and then from out
the poor houses in the vicinity the population darted
and asked questions.

There was a little crowd of ragged Jews round

Kindness of the Jews

each cart, and the wounded sat up and talked, those who could sit up. The Jews brought white rolls, and laid them in the straw by the soldiers' sides, and they put cigarettes in the soldiers' mouths and lit them—many of the soldiers had no use of their arms. Poor wounded, their brown blankets were soaked through, their voices hoarse with cold, their faces pinched and bloodless—but they tried to chuckle and laugh and tell us how they had been beating the Germans! And the crowd cried, one by one, "Have you heard of ours?" "Have you heard of ours?" For the Jews also have their kin in the battle.

The Russians have driven the Germans back from all this country of the Nieman Valley. It was difficult fighting from Insterburg to the Nieman and back again, but retreating or advancing the Russians showed themselves superior to the Germans in courage and verve and military resource. They had to fight against a better equipped army, an army a hundred times better educated, against better guns and better science, but won by virtue of the personal religion in the soldier, and the overwhelming moral justness of the cause. "Thrice is he arm'd that hath his quarrel just."

The Russians got as far into East Prussia as Allenstein at the beginning, of the war. They won battles, they ravaged the country, they sent a rumour of terror before them to Berlin. But they walked into many traps, lost great numbers of men, and blazed away a great quantity of precious ammunition. Impetuous General Ranenkampf, whose brother is a German general on the other side, in fact Governor of Königs-

berg, is reported to have said: "Cut my right hand off
if we are not in Berlin by Christmas." Berlin was a
long way to go, especially for the brave but simple
Russians. Many hard days and retreats and terrible
sanguinary battles were in store, and Christmas in the
trenches—in trenches mostly dug in Russian earth. An
enormous number of Russian prisoners were taken at
the battle of the Mazurian lakes near Oesterode. A
man in Königsberg watched the Russian prisoners
march past for four hours and three-quarters. Many
officers were killed, several generals, and a multitude
of common soldiers. The German General von Hin-
denburg was greatly honoured, the Germans mightily
elated. The Grand Duke Nicholas and his armies were
chased out of Germany altogether, and the hot German pursuit did not cease till the Russians turned at
bay fifty miles to the Russian side of the frontier.

The Germans doubtless were much cheered by the
Russian disappearance, and it was a great thing to be
able to tell their public that not one of the enemy remained on German soil. But their victory was also a
delusion. They in their turn underestimated the strength
of the enemy, and dreamed perhaps of taking Vilna on
the rush.

Or perhaps they sought to divert Russian attention whilst they developed their forces for the attack
on Warsaw and for the relief of Pshemisl. In any case,
their sharp defeat on the banks of the Nieman could
hardly have entered into their plans. They pursued the
Russians back to the Russian bases—keeping to the high
road and to the railroad, and concentrating all their efforts
to gain the other side of the Nieman, and so pierce the
centre of the defence. But the Russians turned and

Impression of the Battle of Sredniki

drove them back, at Simno and Sredniki and Druskenniki and Sein, villages to the north of Grodno. One who watched the battle at Sredniki tells thus of the struggle

"It began to be said that the enemy were nearing us in immense strength, and that they would attack us at the fording of the river. At three in the afternoon the firing began, and in an hour fighting became general, all efforts of the Germans being concentrated on that point of the river where it is joined by the tributary, the Dubissa. On the steep cliff of the right bank moaned the Russian howitzers; down below on the sand of the river shore the field artillery was at work; and on the other side of the river, covered by the artillery fire, the Russian foot heroically repulsed the Germans, who for their part were making superhuman efforts to break through to the shore. The battle was fought all night—right till the dawn. The sounds of the quick-firing guns and of the cannon and the rifle shots mingled in one long, uninterrupted thunder roll the whole night long. But twice above the tumult was heard from afar the cheering of the Russian regiments charging the enemy and driving them back. The fires from burst shells lit up the field of battle, and from many little hills and cliffs of the district it was possible to look down on the conflict, and see it as clearly as if it were being enacted on the palm of the hand.

"At the faint light of dawn the fighting became less vigorous and gradually died down, and there succeeded a strange silence, broken only by occasional rifle shots and far-away shouts. The air still throbbed and thrummed as with a metal voice, but the thunder of battle had ceased. The Germans fled with the night, leaving behind on the battlefield heaps of corpses, shells, broken wagons, automobiles, motor-bicycles. The sun came up brightly, and silvered with his beams the waters of the Nieman, the yellow-leaved drooping forests, the gentle hills, and the extraordinary battlefield. There, where dogs howled and innumerable ravens croaked and fluttered, lay thousands of dead, face downward, face uppermost, some as if they were sleeping, others as if searching to find something in the earth, in heaps, in the trenches, behind mounds, mixed up with guns and swords and helmets. So the sun saw what had happened between his going down and his rising again."

The Tsar sets out for the front, and with the excitement of his possible advent at any point the efforts of generals and officers and men are doubled. So the Germans are driven back, once more the Russian troops cross the frontier.

The Militia is called out to stand in guarded occupation of the country whilst the eager troops press on.

The refugees return; in many cases to ruined homes, burned farms, and sacked villages, but they do not weep over it. "A month ago I was a rich man," said a Pole to me. "I had a large *pension* establishment on the Nieman, and many people came to me for their summer holidays. Now I have nothing but what I stand in, you see. Still, I'll build it again. If the war stops, I'll borrow money and build it again."

AN AEROPLANE HUNT AT WARSAW

THE aeroplanes sail in and out of the light clouds, their stately progress like that of cranes passing over high mountains, and down below, on all the street corners of Warsaw, people stand and gaze at them all day long, pointing, gesticulating, looking through field-glasses. Suddenly, one of these human birds in the sky stops in its steady flight and staggers and falls, and a thousand people in the city below see it falling.

All at once there is a great rush and many cries—"This way is quicker, this way quicker!" and everybody rushes in the straightest line possible for the point where it seems the flying-machine had fallen. A moment before in the street people were merely walking past, or standing and staring; a moment later every one was running in one direction as if possessed.

Out of the restaurants and the cafés dashed the officers having their dinner and with them their ladies, and jumped into waiting motor-cars and followed the crowd. Every cab was taken. People crowded on to every vehicle going in the right direction, and there were many droshkies having as many as a dozen or fifteen passengers standing on them. I was running with my knapsack on my back. Street after street we traversed the farther we went the denser the crowd: Out of the houses came women without their hats, and many children. Policemen left their posts, hawkers their stalls, barbers came out in their aprons, Jews ran in their square hats and black cloaks, students, schoolboys, fifty thousand of them, increasing every moment. When we came to a cul-de-sac, some climbed the palings and ran across unoccupied building plots ; others went round and were in time to race the paling climbers at the other end. It was a regular steeplechase.

Motors went coughing by, hooting with their sirens, tintinnabulating, trumpeting. Horsemen pranced alongside. Only half the people knew what they were after. A panting, breathless student ran past me carrying a T-square in his hand, but having no hat on his head. He relapsed into a walk, and stopped to ask me what was the matter, he for his part had not the least notion !

After about two miles, we issued from the city and came on to the open plains of Poland, and there lay the Russian Army encamped outside the city. Here a Russian aeroplane was making a tremendous clatter just overhead, and the crowd below was running this way and that to avoid a possible bomb that might be thrown at them. They could not be sure that it was not a German aeroplane.

Here we all turned up, on foot, in wagonettes, in motor-cars, on bicycles, girls, boys, men, and women—and came to a standstill.

Where were the fallen aeroplane and the presumably dead Germans ? Nobody knew.

Some rushed this way, some that. Some said: "It's over there " ; others, "it's over here." There was plenty of room, and we all swarmed over the plain as if we had come out for a picnic. The Cossacks from the encampment pranced about. The crowd did not feel very disappointed. Something was going on somewhere. I jumped a trench full of wet mud and climbed on to

Cossacks Chase Back the Warsaw Mob

the rampart opposite. It was crowded with people all the way along, all disputing the merits of the situation. One man held that a bomb had been thrown from a German aeroplane. Another declared that there had been a duel in the air. A third, a Jew, maintained that the Russians, not knowing their business properly, had shot down one of their own aircraft.

The Russian officers looked with astonishment on the crowd that had come out and invaded their territory. Suddenly an order was given to the Cossacks: "Chase all these people back again!" Whrr-pp! Six Cossacks brought their horses round and started forward in a gallop together.

The mob screamed and bolted. Never have I seen such a rush. They went like blown leaves. It was difficult, however, to get down quickly from the rampart. A Polish girl near me tripped, and dived head foremost into the mud in the trench and lay there a minute as in a comic picture. When she crawled up the bank the people stopped in their flight to laugh at her, for her face was covered with yellow mud and wet mud was dripping from her nose.

But it was not a pogrom. The Cossacks were kind, and the crowd of skedaddling black figures laughed as well as screamed. Then more Cossacks came up and started driving us back in earnest. Those who had come in cabs jumped back and ordered the drivers to take them home again, and the motors swung round and bore their would-be sightseers away. Those on foot followed, the whole 50,000 of them and more, flocking, rushing, still asking questions — "What was it? Have the Germans come? Only an aeroplane? Whose? No, never?" and so on. As we went back we met hundreds and thousands on their way to the fields. They also asked—"What is it? Where is it?" And we cried—"Back! back!" And some said—"The Cossacks are coming!" and others said —"The Germans! the Germans!"

Still fatuous crowds gathered round, simple people who were asking one another what was the matter, and those on the outside pushed and punched and strained to see the corpses they thought were in the centre. Even the police were befooled into cutting their way through these onion-like masses to see what was in the centre. But they were onion right through.

I got back to the place I started from. But all the rest of the evening in Warsaw crowds kept forming round people supposed to be "in the know." And still you heard the question—"What was it happened this afternoon?"

The true answer was that a German aeroplane had been shot down by the Russians, and came to earth ten miles away.

That evening all trains going south or west were cancelled. The Vienna station was shut up. The Governor issued a notice asking the people to remain calm, since the troops would defend Warsaw to the last drop of blood. The newspapers held that Warsaw was calm and confident. Next day, Sunday, the faint sounds of distant firing were heard. Crowds went outside the city and heard the sounds more distinctly. They also saw the wounded being brought in.

On Monday we listened to the desultory thunder of cannon. Going to the city to post my daily letters, I found every post-office was closed and was informed that the post had retired to Moscow. I went across the Vistula and out to the suburb of Praga. There was a

A Polish Political Play

post there, but everything had to be written in Russian and the Censor must initial it. Letters could be handed in at 11 p.m. I got nothing through.

On Tuesday, the British, French, and Belgian Consulates closed their doors, the banks shut, scarcely anyone would give change for paper money. There was no bread in the bakers' shops, scarcely any milk to be obtained at the dairies—at the cafés only black coffee. The cannon sounded much louder. The papers held there was no cause for alarm. All the same, removing vans began to appear in the streets. Many shops remained padlocked all day; other shops started sales.

On Wednesday the fighting was more continuous and insistent. It lasted all night, and it was difficult to sleep for the sound of the cannon. The schools were dismissed. The Government theatres closed. The people left the city in great numbers and swarmed literally on to the roofs of trains going to Moscow and Vilna. The Governor issued a notice, posted on all the walls—"Anyone injuring the telephonic or telegraphic connections will be shot *without trial*." Enormous crowds waited at the Vienna station and listened to the battle going on beyond the city.

I went to a little Polish theatre and saw an amusing political comic opera, in which figured William as Alexander of Macedon and two twin German generals, both as Napoleon; the other characters were Miss Warsaw, Moses, a Jew, a French soldier, a Highlander in a kilt, a Russian bogateer, and Austria, a scantily dressed woman, with brass cases over her breasts and a black eagle painted between; on her head was a brass casque and she danced the tango with the Kaiser. One of the funniest things of the evening was a Pogrom Dance performed by the Kaiser. First a girl came in and danced a Polish dance.

Russia and the World

Then the Kaiser jumped up and roared, "Away with that; accept our German culture." Then four marionette babies were fixed on the stage and the Kaiser did a War Dance round them, threatening them with his sword and roaring. When it was all over the Allies marched past singing the Polish Marseillaise. The audience stood up and cheered and cheered again, calling back the dancers and actors to repeat the rarely sung anthem. As a background to the cheering and singing was the never-silent rumble of the cannon.

All night and all next day the cannon sounded more and more threatening, and we began to ask ourselves when would shells begin to drop in the city. Our thoughts were turned in a different direction, however. On Thursday night an aeroplane sailed over the city and dropped a bomb which fell in Wolf Street, destroyed the top storey of a tobacconist's shop, and shattered sixty or seventy windows. On Friday morning crowds turned up here to look at the torn roof and ruined walls and windows. A policeman arrested me as a suspicious character, and I had to go to the police station and satisfy the *preestaf*. This was the third time. *Nitchevo!*

In the afternoon, after dinner, I went into my hotel room and lay down and read the papers. Presently I began to consider the cannonade and ask myself the significance of the increasingly loud reports, when suddenly there was an overwhelming splashing explosion just by. I rushed out again. People were running hither and thither, and overhead was a German aeroplane. Soldiers fired volleys at it; the public, in fright, tried to avoid being directly under the machine. No one could say where the bomb had fallen. We watched the aeroplane fly away unhurt. I went at once to the

"Don't wait upon the order of your going"

Vienna station, and was within one hundred yards of it when another explosion occurred, and the crowd of sightseers came running towards me. This time four soldiers and four horses had been killed, just at the station. The mob was panic-stricken, howling and shrieking. As I stood by a telegraph pole, a girl in hysterics clutched my overcoat, and yelled. "There's not the slightest danger," said I. But as some hundreds of soldiers started firing into the air, she broke into sobs and threw her arms about.

The aeroplane kept fairly low and went along Marshalkovsky, the Piccadilly of Warsaw, and as it went it seemed to drive all manner of traffic along with it. A general in a motor-car came up and shouted to the people, "Home! Home! Don't wait upon the order of your going . . ." It was a *mauvais quart d'heure* for Marshalkovsky. But presently the aviators, after daringly returning and circling over the station, turned away westward and got back to the German camp. The crowds returned to their old standing places, and there began a murmur of conversation that filled whole streets. Warsaw is certainly a city that can be terrorised. On the whole, there was more to fear from the running crowd than from the German "bombists." The roll of the cannon goes on. If the Germans came in there would be a bad state of affairs, but in order to come in they have to defeat an immense, brave Russian army. It is also a matter of the effectiveness of the big German guns. When the weather turns wet, it is difficult to get these guns along. If it remains dry and clear, as to-day, there is bound to be more trouble. As I revised these lines, there was quiet again. The Germans had been defeated. The bombs were their parting shots.

THE FIRST BATTLE OF WARSAW

ON the Sunday after the aeroplane hunt in Warsaw I saw the climax of the great battle that foiled the first German attempt on the city.

The German force that ran the Russians back from East Prussia to the River Nieman, and which was in turn driven back by the Russians, had evidently not been a strong one, and its operation on Russian soil was only a diversion. Whilst Russian attention was fixed on North-West Poland a really important development was taking place in South-West Poland. Here the German and Austrian armies were accumulating and rolling out like a rising thunderstorm on the horizon of Warsaw. Of course, directly the Germans were driven back in the north one looked to the angle where lie Cracow and Breslau for the next big fight, but it only needed two days to show that the Germans and Austrians were coming forward from their own territory with great celerity.

The whole of South-West Poland had been overrun —Chenstokhof, Petrokov, Radom, Ivangorod, and Lodz had all been taken. But for the fact that it is necessary to keep this great nervous mixed population of Warsaw calm, considerable mention of these facts must have been made in dispatches. The German advance on Warsaw nullified for the time being the Russian successes on the road to Cracow. It caused a general retirement of the Russians in Austria. Even Lemberg was in danger for a while. A glance at the railway map will show how important is Warsaw, holding as it does all the network of lines in its grasp. The successive attempts of the Germans to take it show how highly they would prize the capture.

On the final Sunday of the first great battle I wandered outside Warsaw and came to a deserted hut, on the roof of which I sat till nightfall watching the fight.

It is a dull Sunday and the battle thunder is incessant, like a sort of persistent resentment. Earth is smoking upward to a grey-red sky. The whole grey western sky has a dull red glow in it, and from the landscape rise volumes of smoke and flames from burning farms, rise circles of white smoke from shells just burst. Autumn is yellow, there is much mud underfoot, the cabbage fields lie all trampled and stubbed, the grey wooden cottages of the Polish peasants are either deserted or are taken up by soldiers for their night quarters. On my right is a trembling wood, on my left lies the grey high road marked out by telegraph poles. None of the public are allowed on it. But military motor-cars tear along it as if racing; reinforcements of foot march along it to the *positsi;* lorries of wounded return slowly along it, going with their sore burdens to the bandaging point at the outer city gate. Anon, the road is empty, and you look along the whole dreary stretch of it from the foreground, where lies the way up to Warsaw, to the west, where it loses itself in dust and vapour and smoke.

From the north come clanging, metallic explosions, which sound as if the cannon thunder were resounding from many metal roofs. From the south come low, bellowing detonations. From the centre come sharp,

Russia and the World

clouting reports that beat the air like doors banged and banged again—the machine-guns' chatter and rattle. The battle rages towards Warsaw from the north-west, the roar and murmur of battle growing and trembling and raging forward. It sounds every now and then as if some enormous machine on wheels were rolling forward ponderously and irresistibly towards the city. Nearer and nearer come the bursting shells. It is fascinating beyond words to watch and listen.

A sentry came up and questioned me, a pleasant, simple fellow, who was not afraid or absurdly suspicious. I showed him my papers, told him who I was, and offered him a cigarette—I keep a supply of cigarettes for stray soldiers—and he was quite cheerful and happy.

"Yours are fighting well," said he, "the English. I heard how they have been chasing the Germans. Even if they do give us a hot time here they won't beat the English. They are a people, they are a great people."

"The Russians are doing splendidly," said I. "You are the only ones to have fought Germany in Germany; we others, poor Belgians, French, English, have been struggling all the time on our own territory."

The sentry smiled. "I was at Soldau and Leidenburg," said he. "After we got past Mlava we went on and on, and found nothing in our way. We had a hot time coming back, though. Their artillery is so fine, and they have so many telephones. We could never rest with our battery. Wherever we took it they found the range and the mark at once."

"What's going to happen now?" I asked.

"Don't know. We've been fighting them ten days now, and we make no progress. They are very obstinate.

The Climax of the Battle

What do they think they are going to do here? They can't take Warsaw."

"Still you retire?"

"In places. There are many spies."

"How far away are the Germans now?"

"There, in the centre, about six versts"—he pointed to the long grey spectral high road. "I was at the front yesterday—that is about two versts from here—and the Germans lie four versts farther."

"And in the North?" I asked.

"There I don't know. Nearer perhaps. There the Germans are advancing. Their left wing was beaten yesterday, but their right received reinforcements and advanced and took possession of an important ridge."

The sentry went on, and I remained with my thoughts and the battle thunder all around. The sentry reported my presence, and in a while a cantankerous but smiling officer of police came and questioned me and warned me off. I walked with him a mile, however, and talked to him. He said the Russians were winning, and yet every now and then he stopped to listen to the rattle of the machine-guns. I could see him trembling. How strange! The sound of battle drew me nearer and nearer, but he evidently would have given anything to be off duty and out of it all. Still, his orders were to calm everybody he met, and he assured me I should see thousands of German prisoners on the morrow.

And I wandered away from him back to the city. It was about five miles to the outer gate, *Zastava*, of Warsaw, and long before I reached it I saw the black masses of the curious and anxious crowd held back there by the mounted police. These were tremulous days for Warsaw.

Russia and the World

It was five miles more to the centre of the city and a restaurant. At last I reached the centre, and there, as ever at night-time, all was gaiety and frivolity, the cafés full to the doorways, the cinema shows glaring as in Tottenham Court Road, the broad pavements crowded with Polish dandies, with elegantly dressed women and ogling girls, with gossiping Jewesses and black-cloaked Abrahams, with hundreds of newspaper hawkers selling, not only Polish sheets, but also *The Times* and *Le Matin*. There are not many English here, but the Poles read English gladly.

I had my dinner and my coffee listening to a selection of ragtimes.

THE DAY OF VICTORY

A DAY of victory or an armistice. Rumour has it that the German left flank has found itself outnumbered at Ivangorod, and the right flank has had to retire. No cannon thunder in the night, none in the morning, but instead the brightest, warmest day of autumn, an unspent summer day found by the thrifty year and offered us in the gloom of Russian October. The sun shone brilliantly, and from all the trees, and in the open spaces from nothing at all, hung long gossamer threads. All Warsaw was waving in gentle gossamer. Violence and war were far from Nature's thoughts.

It is the Monday after my day out in the country listening to the great battle. I have been down to the Brest station, where the trains go out to Moscow. It is blocked up with fugitives and their hurriedly packed household effects. The more thunder of war and the more bombs thrown from the air, the more people resolve to flee. It is not, however, easy to flee; a special permit has to be obtained and then a ticket. You may wait all day and still fail to get a place on the train. The authorities close the booking, office directly they have sold the places on the two outgoing trains.

On my way back I had a passage of words with a policeman in black and red and his officer in buff. They

Russia and the World

wanted me to go to the police station and be verified again. That was because I am tall and have my tramping boots on, and look unusual. They ought to know that spies are short and inconspicuous. There is, however, said to be an enormous amount of spying being done and a day does not pass but some are hung or shot.

About three o'clock in the afternoon I got back to the great high street of Warsaw—Marshalkovsky—and, as chance would have it, saw another bomb come down and explode. As I walked down the street I suddenly noticed that passers-by began to shade their eyes with their hands, and look up into the sunny sky, and I looked with them.

A great bird was hastening forward over the city—the shape of a German eagle breasting the air. It approached with great rapidity and was soon over our heads. The people began to run, now to this side of the road and now to that—and I myself crossed over. Two moments later there was a flash of smoky fire and a deafening report. Lumps of roof flew into the roadway three doors up from where I was standing; a bomb had fallen on the top of my favourite café, the place where I had sipped my coffee and written my articles so often.

Having discharged the bomb, the unpausing aeroplane went straight on across the vault of the sky and disappeared.

An enormous crowd gathered round the café and talked and questioned. But presently out of the horizon into which he had disappeared came the Prussian eagle once more and approached with similar velocity. There was a great panic in the street, an astonishingly tremulous moment. Even soldiers darted into imaginary shelters, the tram-drivers were afraid to go forward with their cars, cabs with their passengers went whither the drivers fancied. Every one had an intimate notion of what it would be like to be blown to bits. Still, we might as well have stood still. The Germans aim the bombs at the crowds or at important buildings, but they do not hit their marks. The bombs fall on the just and unjust with cheerful impartiality. The one we now feared fell two streets off with a hollow boom, and killed and injured six people who did not even realise there was one of the enemy overhead.

It is difficult to see what the Germans hope to gain by these isolated adventures. Bomb-throwing will not help them either to take the city or to keep it when taken. The Russians know how to keep the nervous population under control in time of excitement, but the Germans, if put in possession of the city, would not be able to restrain the dangerous element, always rather strong in submerged Warsaw.

These single exploits are merely thrill-producers. The "bombists" killed and injured fifty-four people one day last week; according to latest accounts they killed and injured twenty to-day. At the Vienna station one bomb explosion broke £1,000 worth of plate-glass. I have no wish to minimise what they did, but what effect did the outrages have on the result of the battle outside the city? Directly the danger had passed, the people came out again, and were chattering and laughing and picking and choosing fragments of plate-glass to keep as mementoes—like children who, on the night of the fifth of November, were a little frightened by the explosions, but who immensely enjoy gathering the squib cases and rocket sticks on the morning after.

On the Tuesday we knew definitely that there was victory. It was a day of the clashing of bells and of hymns of praise. Warsaw had been saved. Yet such a wet and dreary day. The silence that succeeded after the days and nights of cannon, thunder, and suspense was strange by comparison. It was a pleasure to realise that the post offices were opening again, that the banks would give out money, that telegrams would be passed more easily, that the Consuls were coming back and the jewellers' shops opening, and yet somehow there was a shade of regret as if Destiny and adventure had passed us by.

This melancholy, however, vanished when in the evening great numbers of troops returned to Warsaw from the battlefield. In the soaking rain along the dark, wide streets the Siberian Cossacks, my friends of the Altai among them probably, and with them the Caucasian regiments, returned at a quick measure. It lasted for hours, but it was not a procession. Every horse was trotting, the military carts jogged along quickly. The men were woebegone, grimy, bearded, soaked. They seemed too tired even to tend their horses properly, too tired to take from the extended hands of the Poles the offerings they made of cigarettes and sweet cakes and bread. They had fought day and night for days, taking the chance of death, and then the chance of death again, and then again, seeing their nearest comrades blasted by shells, stricken by bullets, yet not having time to reflect even on what it meant to lose so dear a friend; subconsciously aware even in the rush of their valorous deeds that at any moment

Lucky Ones

fruitful chance might strike them down from the ranks of the striving and living to the heaps of the dead. They were all lucky ones, though perhaps in their philosophy happiest of all were those who perished in the love and service of Russia in the war against an evil foe.

SUFFERING POLAND : A BELGIUM OF THE EAST

SO the first battle of Warsaw was won by the Russians and the Germans were driven back, and nearly all the exchanges and minor engagements following that battle were in the Russian favour. By all accounts, it was the enthusiasm and daring of the peasant soldiers that saved Warsaw from bombardment and German occupation.

The struggle over the body of Poland will rage backwards and forwards for a long time, and the sufferings of the soldiers on both sides and of the non-combatants will be something unparalleled. War is raged with a more elemental brutality on this side of Europe, for the reason that the land was a poverty-stricken one to start with, and because the Russian troops are more used to cold and hunger, more humanly persistent, more unsparing of themselves. Already Russia must have lost heavily, but the losses mean little to her. She is the men-millionaire who never feels poorer, however many men she may spend. The peasants themselves are deeply calm regarding the spectacle of suffering and death. Death does not horrify them ; on the contrary, the idea of glorious death is spiritual meat and drink to them. They love their brother soldier alive, but when he is dead he becomes something holy. This makes the Russian almost invincible. The only thing that could

German Squeamishness

disturb the enthusiasm of the Russian troops would be the idea that they were fighting for a wrong cause. Cannon is not their *ultima ratio*. The technical superiority of the Germans, who were ready for war at all points, is opposed and held in check by the religious bravery of the Russian peasants, and by the spirit that prompts them to think that every battle can be won at the point of the bayonet.

But to turn a moment from the struggle of Slavs and Teutons, there is another spectacle that claims attention, and that is the sufferings of the body of Poland, over which these terrible struggles are taking place. The condition of the peoples of Poland is almost as bad as that of the Belgians. There is only the difference that Belgium was a prosperous and happy country to start with, and Poland for the most part was miserable and poverty-stricken.

When the Germans first invaded Poland they gasped at the filth and poverty of the ghettoes, at the little shops where there was nothing worth stealing, at the wretched houses crammed with humanity, but devoid of wealth and luxury. They surveyed the ragged, shivering Jews with horror, and rather than loot their houses they set them afire. In the first month of the war Poland suffered more from fire and lead than from robbery. Indeed, even the border frays ceased for a while, and all German attention was given to the Russian invasion of Eastern Prussia.

It was only after the retirement of the Russians that Poland began to suffer seriously. Every one had been lulled to confidence by the Russian advance towards Königsberg, and when the great retreat began the pursuing Germans came upon many Polish towns at the most unexpected moment. The people, wakened up in the night by the fire and tumult and thunder of war, rushed from their beds into the streets, got into the line of fire and were killed and injured in great numbers. The panic was terrible. Many thousands of people left their homes and fled, without plan, without counsel, into the wild country. There at this moment are starving Poles and Jews in great numbers wandering about, lost, shot at, accused of being spies, arrested, liable to execution. Some have managed to get into trains and have gone to the cities of the interior. Warsaw alone has 50,000 homeless refugees, and probably every city of Russia has at least Poles, if not Jews, in its hospitable care, besides a number of wounded soldiers.

When the Germans pursued the Russian Army back to the river Nieman and advanced and occupied South-West Poland, they were bent on revenge. They looked no longer disdainfully on the filth and poverty of Poland. Orders had evidently been given that everything serviceable was to be removed from the country —that no rag that might give warmth to the German soldiers in the winter campaign was to be left untaken. Following the German Army came an innumerable train of light wagons, at first almost empty, but at last filled —by the process of taking from her who had naught even that which she had. At the retreat of the Germans from the Nieman, the Russian airmen remarked on the hundreds and thousands of wagons full of stolen goods traversing the country towards Germany, like a sort of dark cloud moving over the surface of the land. Germans, dead on the battlefield below Warsaw, were found to be wearing the clothing

Polish Peasants Bury their Boots

of Polish peasants under their uniforms. Some were found wearing Russian boots, and many carried women's cotton shawls and flannel petticoats.

In many of the villages in Poland the people have buried their boots and spare clothes, with their money, and you are astonished to see the Polish peasants going about with bare feet or in straw slippers. They say that the German soldiers come and pull the boots off their feet to put into their forage sacks. Alas! the Germans are as keen as terriers at finding things that have been buried, and the peasants when they return to villages forsaken a week before, find that their things have all been dug up and taken away. Necessarily, scarcely anyone is earning any wages. The factories are all closed owing to the lack of coal. Even in Warsaw you rarely see a chimney-stack with smoke issuing from it. And time has been spared by the Germans to ransack the warehouses of the industrial cities. An onlooker at a large sugar factory saw almost a thousand tons of sugar removed in one-horse wagons, for instance. At the town of Bzhedin, a sweated labour settlement where man, woman, and child work all day at the sewing of ready-made overcoats, trousers, and so forth, the Germans took off the whole stock, and were as pleased as if they had won a battle.

It is robbery, but the sagacious Germans disguise it as purchase, giving in exchange for the requisitioned clothing cheques printed in the Russian language and payable by the Russian Government. It is hoped that the Jews especially will worry the Russians by trying to get some recognition of the losses they have sustained. But the Jews, much as they abhor the Russian rule, are true to the Government on the whole, and start no propaganda likely to favour Germany. The Germans inspire them with terror. A touching story is told of the Jews of Avgustof. The Germans came towards Avgustof on a Saturday, and the poor Jews there are of the most pious type, who do not light their fires on the Sabbath, do no work, and certainly do not travel. All the Christians fled. The Jews in consternation appealed to their Rabbi for a reading of Holy Writ on the point. The Rabbi not only sanctioned their departure, but showed them an example by going first. So, last of all, the poor Jews crept out with little bundles containing what they felt they must take with them. Each Jewish family has something valuable in the shape of the metal candlesticks which they light on Friday night. Then the Germans came into the town. The saddest sights in Warsaw and Vilna and Kief are the clusters of poor, homeless Jews just come into the city with all that remains to them in their hands.

Of those who have remained behind or who have been overtaken by the German invasion many have been killed, many maimed by the bursting of shells. Many have had their houses burned over them. Many have been executed by the Germans as spies. Many have died or have become crazed through fright. In several towns the Germans fixed up at the street corners corpses of well-known citizens, in order to warn those who remained behind against betrayal. At Chenstokhof the soldiers cut out the famous picture of the Virgin from the ikon-frame and replaced it with a portrait of the Emperor William. This is an example of grim German pleasantry. They have hanged alleged spies on the roadside crosses and peasant shrines of the highway. And they have also scattered from aeroplanes proclama-

The True Neighbours of the Poles

tions to the Poles to the effect that the Poles should trust them. But the Poles having fallen among thieves have little difficulty in deciding who is truly their neighbour. Russia is doing all she can to help this poor, stricken people.

THE CENSORSHIP

IF there is one city more than another that has had plentiful topics of conversation it is Warsaw. Rumours have fled along her streets every day. Not once or twice panic has possessed her utterly. Three times at least before the end of the year it has been threatened with German occupation; three times the Germans have been beaten and hope has again danced in the breasts of the Poles.

I think perhaps it would have been better to let the people of Warsaw know, daily, the facts of the Russian retreats. Surprises are bad for the nerves, especially the surprise of waking up one morning and hearing the cannonade of the enemy at the gates of the city—of the enemy you thought were at least a hundred miles away.

Not only do the Warsaw newspapers omit the facts about their city, but the newspapers of Moscow give daily more details of the state of Warsaw than the actual Warsaw papers themselves. The post may be closed for days, all telegrams may be refused, and yet, daily, Moscow has intelligence and prints it.

This is effected by a simple device. The Warsaw correspondents write out their articles and paragraphs, make up a packet, take it down to the Brest station, and bribe one of the guards of outgoing Moscow trains to take it to the old capital and either post it or deliver it there.

The Rise in the Value of Truth

Necessarily, the Censor in Warsaw under martial law is much more strict than the Censor in Moscow. Still, when the Moscow papers arrive two or three days after their publication in Moscow and begin to be sold in the Warsaw streets, the Censor begins to pass the reprint of news from its columns.

The morning sheets of the city are kept up with titbits such as, "Since the outbreak of the war many more male children than female are being born. The ratio in Warsaw hospitals is about ten to three of boys to girls. This is thought to be Nature's effort to put right the great waste of male lives."

I read: "The events of the last few days have awakened the curiosity of the local population, and every one is trying to learn the freshest news from outside Warsaw. So, behold the appearance of 'walking news-papers'! Frequenters of the cafés know the type, who give much information just obtained from the most reliable sources. Many people give credence to these stories, and hence arise and spread all manner of fables."

This was in the *Warsaw Morning*, a paper that gave no facts whatever; and no matter what happened in the city, what sound of fighting was heard, how many dead bodies came floating down the Vistula, yet insisted that nothing was happening.

During the war many things have risen in value as a result of scarcity, and the chief of them is truth. The censorship is used not only to keep secret military operations, which is its legitimate function, but also to hide from the public all pictures of failure. It degrades journalism almost to the position of paid propaganda. Not only are failures slurred over and defeats covered by euphemisms, but the successes of the other side are

G   81

minimised and laughed at, and their ability to hold out is foolishly under-estimated. Commanders invite journalists to lend their pen to the cause.

The best way to help the cause is by giving the truth and stating doubts and fears as well as hopes and vaunts. The Censor is justified in eliminating panic-striking impressions, or the unredeemed horrible facts of carnage. But he is not justified in suppressing the quiet penetrative thoughts of men who are necessarily calmer in their souls than those who are in the thick of the fighting. The suppression in Russia of the *Russkoe Bogatstvo* and *Zaveti*, radical and troublesome reviews though they be, is, for instance, a little unfortunate. Least of all is the Censor justified in permitting the campaign of vulgarity by which the minds of the rabble are being poisoned. The Germans are not clowns, not vermin, not stupid, not ridiculous. They are an extremely well-educated, intelligent, serious people. Even if in the long run we overcome Germany, and humiliate her, we ought to know clearly what the Germans were, and how it was they were thus beaten.

The Germans are a marvellously patient race to whom the English owe much of what is hardest in themselves. The English are, on the whole, the justest, fairest, kindest people the world has seen; that is what the Union Jack means—fair play, honour, share and share alike. The Russians are a singularly noble, wild, and simple people. Their soldiers, though capable of excesses, are yet the purest-minded, most religious people in the war. And yet Germans, English, and Russians are hideously and vulgarly depicted in the minds of the common people of the hostile nations. War itself is stern and noble, but the low campaign of those whose

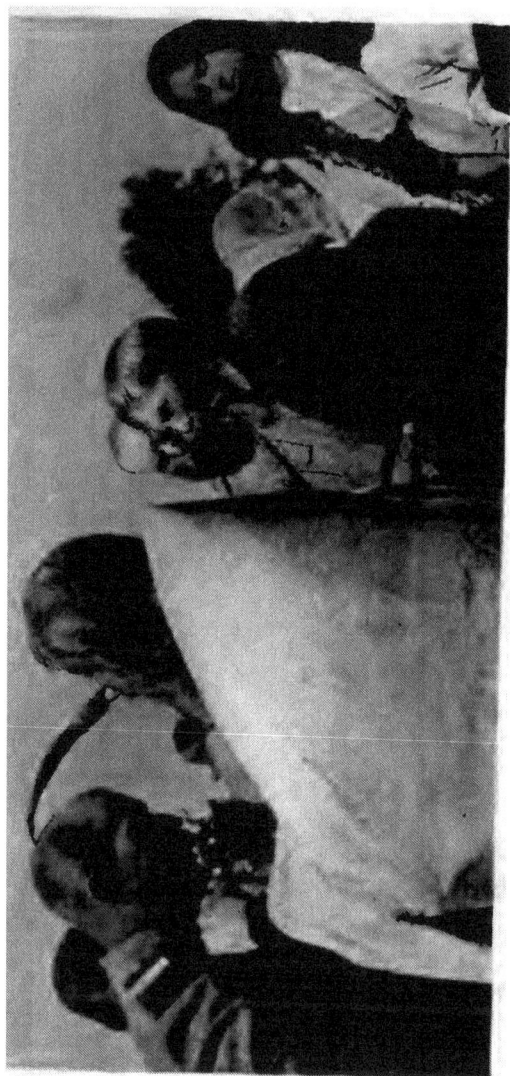

Making the sign of the Cross with holy water on each Cossack's head. The priest is using a paint-brush.

What the War should Mean to Literature

minds run to slanders only brings it into ugliness. So many men dead, so many dying, so many suffering agonies, so many toiling forward towards death, so many lost sweethearts, lost husbands, lost sons, so many tears and prayers, should solemnise the time, and give us, nationally, a noble and restrained literature.

THE SOLDIER AND THE CROSS

WHEN the wounded soldier is brought to the hospital and laid in his bed, his first wish is that the priest may hold the cross for him to kiss. The priest who visits every bedside every morning carries a little cross in his hand, and each poor soldier presses his lips to the centre of it and kisses it vehemently.

War, to the Russian soldier, is a great religious experience. "He liveth best who is always ready to die," says a holy proverb of the Russians. And readiness to die is the religious side of war. The Russian soldier kills his enemy without religious qualm, yet without hate. He does not feel he is doing an evil thing to a fellow man—to shoot at him, to charge at him with a bayonet. The great reality that confronts him is not that he may kill others, but that he himself may suffer terrible pain or may lose the familiar and pleasant thing called life. In order to face this the Russian has to dive down deep in himself and find a deeper self below his ordinary self; he has to find the common spirit of Man below his own ego, he has to live in communion with the fount of life from which his own little stream of life is flowing. No relic of the war is more precious than the little loaf of holy bread which the soldier saves from his last communion before going to battle or going under fire for the first time.

The Russian soldiers go to war very much in the

The Last Communion

same spirit as the Russian pilgrims go towards Jerusalem. Indeed, many a man was just about to start out for Jerusalem when the war broke out and he was summoned to fight against the Germans. In the fields of East Prussia and of Poland he found as veritable a Jerusalem as that he sought in Palestine. It is perhaps a shorter way thither.

The priests serving in the army and in the hospitals tell wonderful stories of religious experience, of touching peasant mysticism, of holy patriotism.

A dying soldier lies on the battlefield and the visiting priest thinks him too far gone to receive the Holy Communion. So he says the *Otkhodnaya*, the prayer for the departing soul. Suddenly the dying man opens his dim eyes and whispers just audibly: "My countrymen, my dear countrymen . . . no, not that, Little Father . . . my own one . . . thou hast come to save me."

He tries to get up, widely crosses himself, that is, from shoulder to shoulder, and from brow to chest, and repeats—"Thou hast come to save me."

There is a short confession as of a child—Communion. The soldier with a great effort crosses himself once more, drops back on the wet mud of the battlefield, and slips into oblivion, with glazed eyes, set lips, but white, calm brow. The priest bending over him lays a cross upon him, and goes on to the next suffering or dying one upon the field.

The Russian religion is the religion of suffering and death, the religion that helps you to meet suffering calmly and to be always ready to die. Many Catholics and Protestants among the Russian ranks ask the Orthodox blessing. In the moment of the ordeal they know that true religion is never divided against itself.

Russia and the World

The war is the great wind that blows through our life, so that the things that can be shaken may be shaken down, and that the things which cannot be shaken may remain. Religion is never shaken down by war. But, strange to say, the logicians are shaken in their logic, agnosticism is shaken, materialism is shaken, atheism is shaken, positivism is shaken. The intellectual dominance is shaken and falls, the spiritual powers are allowed to take possession of men's beings.

"Many is the time," said a priest to me, "that an officer has called me to his side and has said, 'I am an atheist, I believe in nothing,' but I have confessed him, and he has emptied his life to me—to the very dregs—and I have put him in Holy Communion, and left him all melted and holy."

When the war is over and we give ourselves once more to safe life and comfortable life, and we believe again that nothing is more precious than human life, many will no doubt lose the remembrance of that true religion which was theirs in the hours when they were face to face with reality. The cathedrals and the churches will not be so full, the priests will relapse into the routine of the revolving weeks of the revolving Christian year. But still we shall not have lost the fruit of the war. The war has touched us as no other event could touch; it has gone deeper, it has got below the skins and surfaces which are affected by ordinary events, and has stirred depths in the soul. In the stress of war parts of our ordinary superficial selves have got carried down into the depths of the soul. Things that lay hidden in the depths have been cast up to the surface. Things long hid have come to light, and will continue to come to light as in life we go through the gamut of ordinary spiritual experience. New

War is the Autumn Wind

passions will be astir in our loves, new flowers will blossom in our arts, new intentions will become apparent in our destiny. We shall read in ourselves and in Man new promises.

I dare to say that this war has been a spiritual experience, not only for individual men, but for Man himself; not only for Man in the branch of the tree, but for Man in the great trunk from which in spirit we branches all proceed.

Away in the depths of Man, and from deeper depths, proceeds the Almighty Will, in whose fulfilment lies the destiny of Man and the destinies of men. And those who live in communion know that this war is no calamity, no axe at the roots, but the great storm wind of autumn. They know that the wind has blown before, and that it will blow again, scattering leaves and branches into the Death Kingdoms, bringing after it tears of rain and sleep and peace and life again—new life.

SCHOOL CHILDREN

ONE of the phenomena which show how popular
the war is in Russia is the participation of the
children in the conflict. There is scarcely a town
school in Russia from which boys have not run away
to the war. Hundreds of girls have gone off in boys'
clothes and tried to pass themselves off as boys and
enlist as volunteers, and several have got through, since
the medical examination is only a negligible formality
required in one place, forgotten in another; the Russians
are so fit as a whole. So among the wounded in the
battle of the Nieman was a broad-shouldered, vigorous
girl from Zlato-Ust, only 16 years old, and nobody had
dreamed that she was other than the man for whom
she was passing herself off. But not only boys and
girls of 16 and 17, but children of 11 and 12 have con-
trived to have a hand either in the fighting or in the
nursing.

Whilst I was in Vilna there was a touching case—a
little girl of 12 years, Marusia Charushina, turned up.
She had run away from her home in Viatka, some thousand miles away, had got on the train as a "hare," i.e.
without a ticket. The conductor had smiled on her and
let her go on. At Vilna, in the traffic of the great
Polish city, she was a little bewildered, but she asked a
passing soldier the way to a hospital; he took her to
one, and she explained to him that she had come to

88

Boy who has the Russian V.C.

nurse the wounded.   At the hospital a Red Cross nurse
questioned her, and she gave the same answer.   The
nurse telegraphed to the little girl's father, and asked
his permission that she should remain in the hospital
nursing the wounded soldiers.   The father gave permission, so little Marusia was allowed to remain.   A
uniform was made for her, and now as the smallest
Sister of Mercy among them all she tends the soldiers
and is very popular.

There was Stefan Krafchenko, a boy of ten, who
said he wanted to fight the Germans, and so was taken
along by the indulgent soldiers.   He was attached to
the artillery, and handed up shells out of the shell
boxes during three battles and came out of all unscathed,
and glorious and happy.   Then Victor Katchalof, a boy
of thirteen, had his horse shot under him and was himself wounded in the leg during the fight against the
Austrians below Lfof.   Constantin Usof, a boy of
thirteen, was wounded by shrapnel at Avgustof.

Perhaps the greatest schoolboy hero of Russia is a
boy named Orlof, from Zhitomir town school.   He
fought in eleven battles and was eventually decorated
by the Tsar with the Order of St. George.   Whilst
reconnoitring he came into collision with a great force
of the enemy.   He lay in a trench with his fellows and
fought all day.   But ammunition ran very low, and
Orlof saved his corps by creeping out in the dark and
finding his way through heaps of corpses to the main
Russian force.   He was under gun and artillery fire all
the time, but he succeeded in getting across and so
saved his friends.

There are many stories of the children left behind
in the towns and provinces overrun by the Germans.

Russia and the World

I give an amusing one. The Polish name for a certain sort of common mushroom is *Kozaki*, and this led to a misunderstanding. A party of German dragoons came along the border of a forest, and, seeing several little children walking hand-in-hand in the woods, they asked:

"Are there any Cossacks (Cossachen) in the wood?"

"Not in this wood," said the children. "But in that forest on the other side of the meadow there are thousands and thousands."

The dragoons galloped off in a terrible fright.

These are but random instances of the active interest of the school children. The Imperial Academy of Science is collecting, and will probably edit and publish, all manner of printed and unprinted impressions of the war, diaries, minor dispatches or authenticated stories of deeds of derring do. When these are issued it will be seen to what an extent the children of Russia have been fighting in this war. In the playgrounds ten years ago war was unpopular. The war with Japan did not fire the minds of the young ones—the children were all agog then with the idea of revolution, so precocious are the young in Russia.

In the humbler and less romantic life of the children who do not run away there is also much that is beautiful. In Moscow each school has its own special hospital. The children support it, visit it daily. Each child is responsible for the linen underclothing of each man. At the sound of the church bell which is rung intermittently in all the cities the children stop their daily tasks, pause a moment, remember the battlefields and the great struggle, and cross themselves.

In this way school life is touched in England also as well as in Russia. In many country places the village

Lord Kitchener Salutes the Baby

church bell rings to remind the people to pray for the soldiers. And in London also, even in the poorest schools, there is true national feeling and an individual tenderness. When I am in England I frequently go down to one school and talk to the children about Russia and tell them fairy stories. So I have little friends away there, and they write to me upon occasion. And I hear from little Winnie Drew and Dorothy Parker, whose brother has enlisted in the Royal Fusiliers, and Lily Straker, who says the war-prayer in school "partly for my father as well as for all the other soldiers," and from Hilda Dunn and one or two others, all knitting gloves and making warm things for the soldiers, each writing a letter to the soldier who may get the warm thing, putting little notes into the thumbs of the gloves, notes beginning, Dear soldier-protector and the like—receiving the tenderest letters in return from the chance receivers of the gifts. Dear children! Dear soldiers!

A nurse was wheeling a baby in a perambulator past Buckingham Palace one day last December, and, as it happened, Lord Kitchener's motor came up at the same time. There was cross-traffic, and the motor stopped to let it get past. And it stopped just opposite the baby.

"Salute, Pat!" said the nurse.

The little one put his wee hand to his brow and saluted. This caught Kitchener's eye. And he gravely returned the salute.

TROPHIES

THE interest in all the little trophies of the war is great. Soldiers preserve ten-pfennig pieces to take home to their wives as if they were gold. Buttons cut off with bayonets from the German and Austrian dead are prized; also regimental facings, bullets extracted by the surgeon from their own or comrade's wounded body, helmets, swords, pistols, and not only these things, but rings and bracelets and watches. Some peasants have a good eye for what is really valuable. The Poles are the proud possessors of great quantities of German lead picked up on the battlefields, and also of fragments of plate-glass picked up on the pavements of their bomb-stricken capital. The newspapers of various cities exhibit many war curiosities in their windows, and thus attract great crowds. Such a curiosity is the following abridged German diary exhibited in the window of the *Russian Word* publication offices in Moscow. It is one of the many interesting journals of the war.

July 31.—War threatens.

August 1 and 2.—Mobilisation. Food disgusting. Extra pay not received.

August 3.—Our detachment, commanded by Lieutenant Zimmer, pursues three spies.

August 4.—We set out for the frontier. Alarming news that a division of Cossacks is breaking through towards Elbing. Everyone most upset. No Cossacks, however, visible. Food impossible.

The Diary of a Prussian

August 5.—Two squadrons of Russian lancers attack us. We do not answer their fire, the distance is too great and cartridges too precious. Each shot should bring down one of these swine. We pass the frontier. The good high road ends and we plunge into a wilderness of sand and stones. Obliged to dismount from bicycle and walk. At Zelun we confiscated seven wagons. I thought to die of laughter. One wagoner absolutely wouldn't give up his wagon and had to be convinced with the butt end of a rifle.

Lieutenant Zimmer ordered me to share with him my last hard-boiled egg. We put our bicycles in the wagons and got on to Lautenburg, where at the Hôtel de Rome we had a decent supper.

August 6.—We occupied a village near Lautenburg. There was a service going on in the church. Suspecting that explosives were hidden there, ten men, including myself, were told off to break up the floor in front of the altar and search. We had dug down to the vaults when alarm was given and we had to return to the main body.

August 7.—We came to Stary Zelun. Destroyed the post office. Threw the telegraph apparatus into the ^water. Local population quite polite to us.

Two pretty girls here . . . fearfully afraid of us . . . Could not make them understand we intended no harm.

August 8.—Information received that a division of Russian cavalry has invaded Prussia towards Neidenburg. We move on towards Ilovo.

August 9.—Sunday. We advanced towards Mlava. South from Ilovo we came under fire. We were in a valley and they shot at us from all sides, shot continuously.

The first to be wounded was Lieutenant Makketanz. Wounded in the brow. 'The second to be wounded was Sergeant Derke. Wounded in the stomach. The third, Lieutenant Zander. Two wounds in the chest. I wonder if he is alive still. The fourth to be wounded was myself. . . . I was on my bicycle and the bullet struck me in the forearm, apparently breaking an artery, for the blood flowed from the wound. I rushed to Sergeant Kaiser, holding the wound tightly with my right hand. Kaiser tied it up. I ran back to shelter. Found Ramsdorf lying in his blood in great pain. I gave him drink.

Sergeant-Major Zink is a great coward. . . . It's not surprising, therefore, that he hid himself. He was afraid of receiving a bullet. Our detachment hurriedly retired. We wounded were left.

In fifteen minutes the enemy appeared. Cossacks. Filthy, but very kind. They carried us away. One of them took possession of my gun. I had, however, taken care to break it before they came.

We were taken to Mlava and treated much better than we expected. Dr. K—— operated on me and was most attentive and polite. I suffered a good deal, not being chloroformed. I was looked after by a very sympathetic volunteer nurse who spoke German extremely well, though she was Russian, the sister of an officer at the war.

To my immense astonishment we Germans were allowed to be together in the hospital and talk as much as we liked.

August 10.—Re-bandaged to-day, since my wound

Clean Underclothing: Glory be to God!

has been giving me great pain. I retain my consciousness. As I lay on the operating table I suddenly wanted beer. I asked for it. Everybody laughed, and I also, because I did not say "bier" in German, but used the Russian word *peevo*. Dr. K—— promised it me, and in an hour I had it.

August 11.—Wakened by noise of shooting. A German aeroplane was circling over the town and the Russians were shooting at it. The aeroplane got away. Thank God!

Learned to-day the name of my beautiful, kind nurse. I shall remember it all my life. We are to be sent to Warsaw. She has promised to let our relatives know.

August 12.—Taken in wagons to the train. The railway carriages are very comfortable.

Next to me lay a Cossack. He was wounded in the chest and moaned all day and all night. When he drank, water ran out at the wound. Our bullets are more vicious than the Russian ones.

At Novo-Georgievsk we changed trains. Crowds of people stared at us, some pitying, some reviling us.

We received clean underclothing to-day. Glory be to God!

August 13.—Food good and plentiful, but life is a bore.

August 14.—Food is good.

August 15.—Re-bandaged.

August 16.—Officers come in and talk to us for a whole hour. It is very gay. We hope that our good sword will win where diplomacy failed. Food good.

August 17.—We still stand at a wayside station. Prussian officer brought in. He has been convicted as a spy. He has an estate in Russia and had entertained German soldiers there. He is to be shot. He charges me to give messages to his sweetheart and his brother.

He was calm and determined.

August 18.—Brought in Lieutenant Riboldt, captured. We are all being sent to Warsaw. The wounded Cossack is dead; we watched his funeral.

August 19.—They say we shall be in Warsaw to-morrow. We shall see! The food is good, especially the supper. We had *Kletsky* last night.

At this point the diary ended.

THE EVERGREENS REMAIN

WHAT days I had at Vilna tramping in the rain! I found myself so much nearer to the war than I had been before. The war became more intimate, it created and released a musical flood of thoughts and impressions, so that all the time I walked I was like Abt Vogler at the organ. The tramp of thousands to conflict and death, the battle music, the passion of war and the dance of the orgy, the colours and the flags, the emblems and signs, the victories and the terrible slaughters, the conquest of kingdoms, the abasing of old gods, and the building of new States, blends in the soul in one great passionate and appalling music.

It seemed I scarcely slept an hour any night of my month in Poland. I lived two or three festival days into each ordinary day, and yet I never grew tired or dull. I often said to myself: This cannot go on; I shall have a reaction against this life, and flee away to some quiet corner in the Crimea or the Caucasus. But the tired moment never came. As Loosha said to me one day when I reproached her for spending whole nights smoking or talking—"Life has become too interesting."

I read one book over and over again whilst I was in Poland, and that was Shakespeare's "Richard III." I had it in my pocket. That is the use of pocket editions. What matter if pockets do bulge; they were meant to bulge with good things. It is a splendid gain for any

man to have for a considerable stretch of time the same
book in his pocket, and to read it over and over again
and so penetrate it, wed it to his life, associate it in
memory with the facts of a time. Walk with Shakespeare or St. John or Robert Browning, or whom
you will—only walk with one of them. They are not
dead: they are lonely ones, they are would-be living
companions.

"Richard III." is a play all about conscience, about
the thoughts and ghosts which rise out of the depth of
the soul and show themselves in our waking or dreaming
hours. It is like Dostoieffsky's "Crime and Punishment"
in Russian literature, and is as charitably written. It gives
the full story of Richard as the other does of Raskolnikof, it does not merely dismiss him as a bad man. In
thinking of the Kaiser whom so many hate, it is well to
have in mind "Richard III." What is more poignant
than that speech of Richard on his last night when he
starts from an evil dream—

> "Give me another horse, bind up my wounds;
> Have mercy, Jesu! Soft! I did but dream.
> O coward conscience, how dost thou afflict me!
> The lights burn blue. It is now dead midnight.
> Cold fearful drops stand on my trembling flesh.
> What do I fear? Myself? There's none else by:
> Richard loves Richard; that is, I am I.
> Is there a murderer here? No; Yes, I am:
> Then fly. What, from myself? Great reason why,—
> Lest I revenge myself upon myself.
> Alack, I love myself! Wherefore? for any good
> That I myself have done unto myself?
> O, no! alas, I rather hate myself
> For hateful deeds committed by myself!
> I am a villain; yet I lie, I am not.
> Fool, of thyself speak well; fool, do not flatter.

A Vision of the Soul

My conscience hath a thousand several tongues,
And every tongue brings in a several tale,
And every tale condemns me for a villain.
Perjury, perjury, in the high'st degree ;
Murder, stern murder, in the dir'st degree ;
All several sins, all used in each degree,
Throng to the bar, crying all, 'Guilty ! guilty !'
I shall despair. There is no creature loves me ;
And if I die, no soul shall pity me ;
Nay, wherefore should they, since that I myself
Find in myself no pity to myself?

　　．　　．　　．　　．　　．　　．

Methought the souls of all that I had murdered
Came to my tent, and every one did threat
To-morrow's vengeance on the head of Richard.

　　．　　．　　．　　．　　．　　．

By the Apostle Paul, shadows to-night
Have struck more terror to the soul of Richard
Than can the substance of ten thousand soldiers
Armèd in proof."

Is anything of its kind more wonderful than the speech of Clarence in the Tower, the telling of the vision that his soul sees—

　　　　　　　　　"then came wandering by
A shadow like an angel, with bright hair
Dabbled in blood ; and he shrieked out aloud,
'Clarence is come'—false, fleeting, perjured Clarence ;
That stabbed me in the field by Tewksbury."

How apt to the occasion of the war are a hundred little phrases in "Richard III."—

"So now prosperity begins to mellow
And drop into the rotten mouth of death."

or Richard's war speech defaming the enemy—

"Remember whom you are to cope withal ;
A sort of vagabonds, rascals, runaways."

99

Russia and the World

Shakespeare and Dostoieffsky remain, and we are glad of them. We love them, though we love also many of the gentler and nearer who, with the coming of war, have become dumb for us.

Some of the best lines in Hardy's "Dynasts" are those wherein he sings of the flowers and butterflies of the field of Waterloo, how they were stamped into blood and mud and destroyed unnoticed in the great human struggle. How many beautiful flowers and winged fancies perish in the hour of lustful and coarse conflict! Not only the flowers and winged beauties of the field, but the more delicate things all the world over. The playing of the lute and the guitar give way to the drum and the cymbal as in turn these give way to violin and organ. The sweet lyrics of peace give way to battle marches and satires, and these give way in turn to odes of victory and hymns to the dead.

A great change takes place in the conditions of culture. The sudden chilly autumn strikes down upon our luxuriant summer and withers it at a breath.

> "We anxious ask, will spring return
> And birds and flowers again be gay?"

But for the hour and the month there is winter and sleep. Only the evergreens keep awake and rustle or dream in the winter wind or peace. So in our culture the evergreens remain.

How dead is modern Russian literature at this moment! English publishing houses, like the quern at the bottom of the sea which is grinding out herrings and soup, are still grinding out novels and travel books; but in Russia, owing to lack of paper, the strictness of the Censor, and the fact that people

Back to Shakespeare and Dostoieffsky

have no 'ears but for the war and Russia, Russian publication has almost ceased. Some of the best magazines, such as *Zaveti* and *Russkoe Bogatstvo*, have been stopped for the reason of the war. The theatres are putting on only old favourites, or else tinsel and war-paint dramas of the type of Leonid Andreef's play about Belgium and its King. The poets have paused. The great ecclesiastical and religious discussions that occupied last year have lost interest. The ugly novels and plays which feed the bourgeoisie have ceased to appear.

In England, and Scotland also, it is noticeable that the war has given us a truer perspective and cleared away the Lilliputian obstructions of modern life. We see Shakespeare great and wonderful again, and our mockers of Shakespeare shrink to figures like those men made of matches that used to appear on Bryant & May's match-boxes.

I suppose all over Europe, with the beautiful flowers have perished also the rank weeds and fungi of autumn. The great tree Shakespeare remains, but the tall, jealous, prickly nettle that grew beside the tree has withered away. The evil toadstools, scarlet with poisonous lure, have disappeared, and the whiteness of the snow has covered them, as it were, with God's mercy. The trampled mud has hardened, and with the season we are glad.

In England and Scotland we are with Shakespeare and Milton and Campbell once more; in Russia, instead of the futurist Severanin or the sex-novelist Artsibashef, they are back with Dostoieffsky and Tolstoy. The rot of autumn has disappeared from both countries, and there is nothing left but to remember the summer and hope for spring—hope for the first flowers after the war.

Russia and the World

There is a great feeling of expectancy in the air even now, a wonder as to what the new flowers will be like—the new revival. Readers are the sunbeams which bring forth out of obscurity the literary flowers. And a new class of readers is coming into being. For all true poets is the divining what it is that is asked of them by these children of the coming age.

RUSSIANS

THE Russian peasant soldier regards the enemy as vermin that must be destroyed. He has no doubt but that he is clearing away something ugly and full of evil. He is fighting something pestilential like the cholera or the plague.

The bodies of the Germans and the Austrians lie rotting on the fields of Poland this autumn and early winter and infecting the air with odours. It was with difficulty that the Russian soldier could be made to understand that he must bury them.

"Bury these corpses," says a general to one of his servant soldiers.

"No, your Excellency," says the latter, "let them lie there like dogs, they are not fit to be buried in the good earth."

When I told some soldiers of the sinking of the *Emden* and the capture of von Müller they could not understand our leniency towards the German captain.

"Such people ought to be destroyed directly they are caught," said one of the soldiers. "He ought to have been executed at once."

In this spirit, of course, the peasant soldier goes forth for the Tsar, to any of the Tsar's work, and whether it be war against Japan, or suppression of the Trans-Caucasian cut-throats in North Persia, or a pogrom of a distasteful race he has much the same outlook. He is so unswervingly loyal to the word of the Tsar, or what is told him is the word of the Tsar.

There has been no bandying of wit between German and Russian soldiers as there is said to have been between German and British. For one thing, the Germans do not understand Russian. For another, the Russian soldiers are carefully trained not to enter into any sort of converse or familiarity with their enemies. During the time of the revolutionary outburst in Russia, it was indeed rather difficult for ordinary Russian civilians to joke or talk with Russian soldiers.

This necessarily adds value to the peasantry as reliable fighting material.

Then the religion of the peasant helps him to be brave. The Russian army on the offensive is something like an elemental destructive force. There is no hesitation about the Russians, little giving of quarter, little seeing of white flags, no malice, no lust, not much delight in cruelty, but, on the other hand, no squeamishness. The blood flowing does not turn the Russian sick, the sight of the dead does not make him pale. He is striking with the sword of the Lord.

True, the principal function and purpose of war is going to kill. And therein lies not only a denial of Christianity, but of the primitive Judaic law, "Thou shalt not kill." But the function of Russian war that has struck me most was that of going to be killed.

When in the Altai Mountains in the middle of the consecration service I learned that it was Germany who had declared war upon Russia, I felt that the consecration was consecration unto death, the strapping of the knapsack on the back was like the tying on of the cross.

The religion of Russia is the religion of death. As I

The Religion of Death

wrote in my book on the Russian peasant-pilgrims journeying toward the Sepulchre at Jerusalem:

> "All pilgrimages are pilgrimages to the Altar, to the place of death. Protestantism reveals itself as the religion of the mystery of life; Orthodoxy as the religion of death."

The Russians march to battle as they tramp to shrines. Death is no calamity for them. It is the thrice beautiful and thrice holy culmination of the life pilgrimage. Watch the Russian soldiers at one of the many funerals of fallen comrades. They are calm and reverent, but it is the calm and reverence that are the accompaniment of an exaltation of spirit.

But the Cossacks are different in their religious temperament. They are the descendants of robber tribes and mercenary bands. To realise what the Cossacks have been you must read Gogol's "Tarass Bulba," * and when you have realised what they were you have a notion of what they are. There is much Russian blood in them, but there is also much of the Tartar and the Mongol. They have not much in common with the gentle Slav. Their conception of Christianity is very different from that which animates the moujiks.

The Cossack is always a soldier. In Cossack villages every man has to serve in the army — only-sons have no privileges. It is rarely that a Cossack is rejected on medical grounds, and rarer still is his acceptance of rejection. By his passport he is a soldier. When he is farming he is said to be "on leave." The village is not called a village but a station, a *stanitza*. Almost every man in the station works in trousers that have a broad military stripe. By that stripe you may tell the Cossacks and the Cossack stations in the country.

* "Tarass Bulba," by Gogol. A translation of this excellent book has appeared in English.

Russia and the World

As I tramped through several hundred miles of Cossack country last summer I have a very bright impression of the people. They have considerable possessions of land. The Government pursues a set policy of giving the Cossacks land, space wherein to live well and multiply. The whole of Central Asia and Turkestan is preferably settled by Cossacks. The Russian Government trains the men for two or three years, and when the time of training has been run through the authorities propose to them that they settle down near the place where they have been encamped. Land will be given them free. They can bring their sweethearts and their wives. The docile Kirghiz and Chinese and other aborigines can be practically forced to build houses for them and dig out irrigation canals and plant poplars and willows. A company of Cossacks accepts the Government proposal and so a new station is marked on the map. A church is built. A horizontal bar and a wooden horse and a greasy pole are put up. A vodka shop is supplied. And that constitutes Cossack civilisation. The vodka shops are now all closed and there is talk of re-opening them as schools.

The talk and the songs and the life of the station are all military. The talks are of battles lately and battles long ago, and the battles of the future; the songs are recruiting songs and war songs; the life is ever with the gun and on horseback.

Children ride on horseback as soon as they can walk and jump. Little boys get their elder brothers' uniforms cut down to wear, the trousers be they ever so ragged have still the broad coloured stripe that marks the Cossacks. Siberian Cossacks have red stripes, Don Cossacks have blue stripes. Marching songs are on the children's

Cossack Christianity

lips, and one of the most frequent sights is that of a company of Cossacks riding up the main street of the *stanitza* carrying long black pikes in their hands and singing choruses as they go. The pike is another distinction of the Cossack; it is a long black wooden lance which is steel-pointed like a spear.

No woman grudges her children to the war. War is the element in which they all live, and the official manœuvres are so wild and fierce that many get killed in them, kill one another even, forgetting that they are only playing at war. The Cossacks even in remote Asia take themselves seriously as the personal bodyguards of the Tsar; formerly robbers and border riders of the wildest type, they are now, thanks to tactful handling, the most loyal subjects of the Tsar, and are bred out on the Seven-Rivers-Land and the Altai Mountains, for instance, much as one might breed a type of horse, for sterling qualities. They are called Orthodox Christians, but have seldom a mystical sense of Christianity. They are much more superstitious than the moujiks. They hand down their ikons and their battle charms from generation to generation and worship them almost idolatrously.

Their homes are neither comfortable nor clean, the homes of eagles rather than of men. The women are less tidy than ordinary Russian peasant women, and eat more and sleep more.

As a fair companion of the road explained to me:

"It's the women must be blamed for the disorder in their cottages. After dinner the women always lie down and fall asleep, and they leave all the dirty dishes on the table and let the pigs and the chickens come in and hunt for food."

Russia and the World

You enter the little room that is all in all of a home, and you find fifty thousand flies flustering over everything. Often of an afternoon I have entered a cottage in order to get milk and have found everyone asleep, even the dog, who but opens one eye at the noise of my step. The baby lies in the swing cradle and tosses now and then, and cries a little. He would be almost naked were he not black with flies. The chickens keep pecking flies off his body and hurting him—that is why he cries. None the less, the baby will grow up to be a sturdy Cossack. The children are none the worse for dirt and disorder, to judge from the fine young men we see, tall, agile, hawk-faced, the rising generation no weaker than the fathers.

They are hospitable, but because of the biting flies I have found it more comfortable to sleep out of doors, even in bad weather, even when mosquitoes were thick. They always give you full measure and running over when you buy from them. But they are altogether left behind in hospitality by their neighbours the Kirghiz or the Mongolians.

The Cossack has settled where of old the Kirghiz had his best pastures. He has harried the gentle Eastern into the bare lands and wildernesses and over the border to China. The winter pastures that the Kirghiz has discovered for himself and marked out with stones the Cossack has pitilessly mown for hay. Even his houses, the long village street of them, the Cossack makes the Kirghiz build, whilst he stands by like a *barin* or a master. The Kirghiz will take lower wages for his labour than even the Chinee; he can be persuaded on occasion to work for nothing.

"You are entering Kirghiz country now; there are

The Cossacks' Way

no Russian villages, no Cossack stations," said one to me. "No matter, you can always spend the night in a Kirghiz tent and you will always get food from them, as much as you want. Don't ever pay them anything. They don't expect it. They will give you the best they have, but don't pay. You needn't. They are that sort of people, *glupovaty*, stupid-like. It is established so with them."

The favourite adjective applied by Russians to Cossack is *otchainy*, which is supposed to mean "desperate," but certainly does not mean it in the ordinary sense of hopeless. It means past-praying-for, wild-beyond-all-hopes.

"The Siberian Cossacks, they are the wildest of all," you'll hear.

They are spoken of by ordinary Russians much as the Highlanders are spoken of by us, and in some respects they resemble the clansmen. They are brave beyond any qualification. They are all expert horsemen, and ride like the wind. Their favourite exploit is to charge to meet the enemy lying close to their horses' sides, even to their horses' bellies, so that it looks to the enemy as if a drove of riderless horses was plunging towards them. And when the Cossacks arrive at the object of their charge, Heaven help the poor Uhlans or ordinary European cavalry and infantry who happen to be in the way. The Cossacks delight in the cutting off of heads.

It was the Siberian Cossacks who turned the scale at the first battle of Warsaw, and with them, as brothers-in-arms, the Caucasian cavalry. The Caucasian tribesmen are, if anything, more warlike than the Cossacks, stronger physically, always wearing arms and understanding life as military gallantry, having much less regard for the value of life, and much more given to fighting in time of peace. Murder has no moral stigma in the Caucasus; the man who has killed another man is not troubled about his crime, not troubled in his mind, not obliged to return and look at the corpse, not obliged to confess at the last. Indeed, many of the pleasantest and most courteous men you may meet in the mountains have several what we should call "murders" to their charge. Their success in fighting gives them more confidence and more politeness.

They are not quite so brave as the Cossacks, being considerably more intelligent and a very calculating people. They consider themselves Liberals, and are not so loyal to the Tsar. They are corruptible, and the Russian system of bribery has been much improved by them. They are more cruel than the Cossacks, less Christian. A fine body of people, however, the handsomest men in Europe, the hardest.

War for them is also the most interesting thing in life, and conversation over the endless stoops of red wine always turns to battles. By the way, the prohibition of the sale of vodka and beer leaves the Caucasus just as drunken as before. The Government had no monopoly there in the sale of spirits. Everyone could sell who wanted to. Vodka, however, was never much drunk, owing to the fact that the Caucasus has its own good vintage, and the natives despise the use of spirits as a sign of lower caste. It is noble to drink wine, base to drink spirits.

They are a poor people as money goes. It is marvellous that they retain their physique considering the poorness of the food they eat and the quantity of wine they drink. Many villages subsist on black bread and wine. They are always hungry. They could live much better than they do. They love clothes, love rich carpets and elegant ornaments. They would put jewels on their wives, would be princes not only in title but in estate, and would hold Court and go out hunting or to battle with retainers in the good old way.

The Finns are another people under the Russian rule, and Finland one more of All the Russias. Their fighting qualities do not call for comment; they are brave men, stubborn, obedient, mostly foot soldiers. Their sympathies are not with Russia, and when left to themselves the people develop a peculiarly Teutonic type of civilisation. They are clean, orderly, thrifty. In a hard climate they have the grace to make the means to live well. They seem to me to be a distinct nation, and might well be trusted to look after themselves. They have already their own Finnish money, their own Finnish postal stamps, the Finnish language is spoken freely, and, indeed, in the villages and small towns it is extremely difficult to make oneself understood in Russian. These are the outward signs, therefore, of a separate nationality.

Russia feels that there is danger in Finnish freedom, owing to the sympathy between the Finns and the Swedes. And the Swedes have been pronouncing very bellicose manifestoes against Russia in the time previous to this great war between Russia and Germany. War between Sweden and Russia has been a political card for some time.*

Still, Finland, despite rumours in the first days of the war, has remained faithful to the Russian Emperor, and has recognised that it would sooner be a Russian than a German province.

* It is very probable that the seeming harshness of Russia towards Finland is due to fear of Swedish intrigue. The local autonomy in Finland is not seriously threatened.

Russia and the World

Russia is pulling all together. No one would have thought it likely that Russians, Cossacks, Georgians, Finns, Poles, and Jews would at any time be fighting together in unanimity. But there it is.

The war has proved a wonderful touchstone for virtue, a divining rod for hidden gold. It has brought out and revealed the hidden qualities in nations and individuals. Many people have held that the Russians were a noble nation, generous, brave and pious. The war has brought their qualities out in such a way that even the accustomed doubter of Russia has been obliged to confess that he may have been wrong.

The war has given faith. Despite the previous horror of war, it is now almost a platitude to praise the war. Even in peace-loving England the war is recognised as a national blessing, certainly in no sense as a national calamity. It has reduced our cranks and celebrities to their true dimensions; it has calmed the noisy Ulster squabble; it has taken our attention off our national ill-health and turned it on our splendid but neglected youth. It has given us a duty to a fatherland and to ourselves beyond the duty to business and position. It has showed us the necessity of drilling and holding ourselves up straight, of being hard, of prizing discomfort and danger. It has made the Empire greater and clearer, and has given the go-by to the cult of go-as-you-please and get-along-somehow.

Unfortunately, among those in England who have no personal stake in the war, no one fighting in the trenches, no one drilling, no one serving on special duty, there is a certain amount of apathy and pessimism. But in Russia there is no apathy. The whole atmosphere is one of eagerness and optimism. They are full of thankfulness for the things the war has brought to Russia—national enthusiasm, national tenderness, national temperance, and moral unanimity. The war has closed the vodka shop; it has healed the age-long fratricidal strife with Poland; it has shown to the world and to themselves the simple strength and bravery of the Russian soldiers, and the new sobriety and efficiency of their officers. It has, in fact, given a real future to Russia to think about; it has shed, as from a great lamp, light on the great road of Russian destiny. Russians have always dimly divined that they were a young nation of genius, they have held faith in themselves despite dark hours; but now they feel confirmed and certain of their destiny, of their progress from being an ill-cemented patchwork of countries to being a single body, feeling in all limbs the beat of a single heart; of their progress from quietness and vast illiteracy to being confident possessors of a great strong voice in the counsels of nations; of their progress from denial and anarchism and individual obstinacy to affirmation, co-operation, and readiness to serve. As nations go, Britain is like a man of forty-five, Germany like a man of thirty, but Russia like a genius who is just eighteen. It is the young man that you find in Russia, virginal, full of mystery, looking out at the world full of colour and holiness and passion and sordidness.

Despite the beauty and self-sufficiency of the old life, Russia is definitely committing herself to the new. She is going to have a Puritan intolerance for sin, she is beginning to manifest that passion for solid education that has marked Puritan Scotland, America, Germany. More and more people are going to take up with materialism and ethics and agnosticism. Not that Russian pilgrimaging or asceticism or religious observance can ever cease, or that the mystical outlook will be lost, but that Westernism and success and national facetiousness and light-heartedness will be so much more clamorous.

I am a great admirer of the popular saint, Father Seraphim. He is the Russian St. Francis—he tamed the bears and the wolves and the birds of the forest of Sarof. He was so holy that bears, so far from hurting him, actually inconvenienced him a little by their officious helpfulness. But his chief claim to holiness lies in his mystical denial of life. He lived alone in the forest, wore a heavy cross on his back, prayed a thousand days and a thousand nights still kneeling on the same stone, he made a vow of silence and did not open his mouth to speak for twenty-five years, and when the end of the twenty-five years came he remained silent for ten years more. Such an act of denial is called a *podvig*.

I spoke of the *podvig* this autumn to Loosha, a woman friend of mine of whom I wrote in "Changing Russia." I was then working to find words for the essential idea of Russia's religion.

"I like to think that even now, in all this noise of the war, you have in the background of Russia men and women who have taken, like Father Seraphim, this oath of silence, who will never utter a word whether Russia wins or seems to be in danger. It is an astonishing fact that St. Seraphim was silent throughout the whole time of the great Napoleonic campaigns, and did not utter a word even in the culminating distress of the capture of Moscow in 1812."

So said I to Loosha.

Loosha replied:

"That is old-fashioned. Seraphim's greater feat and that which did indeed make him a holy man, was when at last he renounced silence, and after thirty-five

years opened his mouth once more to converse, not
oracularly, but kindly and cheerfully and wisely with
his fellow beings. I think Spring is a greater victory
than Autumn. It is a victory over death, whereas
Autumn is a victory over life."

To this, Western minds will readily give assent. It
is a purely Western idea. But it is a new feeling in
Russia. A few years ago Loosha was of opinion that
she herself was really dead, and that the woman who
spoke to me was but a shadow, a ghost, something
without warmth, without heart, without hope. She was
glad to have conquered life. Now she wants to conquer
death and win again.

Russia the silent one, silent for twenty-five years,
and then silent for ten years more, is either speaking
now or is about to speak. The spirit moves mysteriously in her. She begins to know that a new time is
at hand.

THE GERMANS

AT Bielostock I met a peasant soldier from Ossovets, a dispatch-bearer. "How are you getting on out there?" I asked.

"They run," said he.

"That's an important victory, isn't it?" I replied.

"Their Emperor was there, somewhere about Ossovets," said the soldier. "If we'd only known in time we'd a taken him."

"But he would have been in a very safe position," I urged.

"Oh, we'd a had him, even if we had lost thousands. If they'd told us, we would have done anything to take him. He's more than a flag—he's their Tsar."

This is the spirit of the Russian soldiers just now. If their officers ask them to take a hill they will take it, or storm a fort against terrible artillery fire, they will storm it. They have got going, they are on the wave of a tremendous national enthusiasm. They fight with cries and shouts, with songs. They have to be constantly reproved for marching too fast, and for treading on one another's heels at the fording of the rivers. They need no band, no banjo to "spur the rearguard to a walk." They are very heavily clad, clumsily shod, burdened with a heavy kit, from which dangle pots and kettles. They live on the most frugal diet, and do not grumble when they starve. They sleep under the open sky these wet, cold nights of autumn. They have the longest patience in the world, and yet they have also an extraordinary verve and eagerness. This is a wonderful combination, emotion on a foundation of patience.

The Germans are stubborn, they are persistent and determined. They are condemnatory and angry, and are capable of a fine rage. They are self-confident and plucky. They are what we English call "nasty." As brutes they have most in common with the wild boar, most vicious and dangerous of animals. On the whole, one would back the Germans against anyone in the world for sheer devilry. One would also back them for their mastery and assimilation of the results of scientific invention and material progress. They are the most accurate and best-equipped people.

But it is not the devil in man that wins in the long run. The devil in man is terrible, but it is the God in man that gives victory and happiness. Nietzsche wrote frequently of the "God, devil, and worm in man," and mistaken Nietzscheanism always tends to the development of the devil in man, exclusive of the other two. The Russian, as Dostoieffsky wrote, is the God-carrier. You must appeal to the religious in him; you must appeal to his emotions. But you have to appeal to the bad temper of the Germans to make them go.

Russians versus Germans is Imagination versus Will. Both will and imagination will carry men far, but imagination will carry farther. For the imaginative soldier has his eyes set on an unearthly prize, and he forgets his body and all the limitations of his body, and goes forward in a state of rapture.

One of the features of the present life of Russia is the going over of a considerable number of Lutherans to the Orthodox Russian Church. I was present at the receiving at the font of two such converts—a most impressive service. They were two women, Russian subjects, but German by extraction. It was evidently a very great event in their lives—their faces were a picture of emotional excitement and childish happiness. I suppose many of us who do not formally enter or fall away from Churches have in spirit made that transference from puritanism to orthodoxy. It is always a tremendous personal event, the transference of religion from the intellect to the emotions, the melting of the ice of personality, the change from a rigid setting of the lips to the filming of the eyes.

Nietzsche, of whom many random things are being said in this the time of our indignation and sorrow, detested the modern German puritans. "When they say I am just, it soundeth as if they had said I am just—revenged. Thus spake Zarathustra." Nietzsche understood that Germany's self-righteousness sprang from a sort of hatred of life and of men.

I am sorry words are being said against Nietzsche. He was one of my teachers; I learned much of him. I am sure many British who have rifles on their shoulders to-day have learned of Nietzsche, and have a warm place in their hearts for him. They have taken his works with them, and Zarathustra in some man's breast pocket must have saved him from an evil ounce of lead.

Nietzsche was of Polish origin, and consequently nearer to the Russian spirit than to the German. Although he seems anti-Christian, he was on the road to transcendent Christianity. He was a great admirer of Dostoieffsky, whose work he introduced to Germany. Nietzsche, always half-mad, alternately possessed by devils and angels, might have been a character in one of Dostoieffsky's novels. For the rest, Nietzsche was very fond of the French people, and preferred to read his own works in the French translation rather than in the original. He greatly admired Stendhal and he abhorred Kant. The spectacle of the genius of Napoleon made life worth living for him; the success of Wagner so mortified him that it must have hastened his madness by ten years at least. He disliked the English, it is true, but that was because it was in England chiefly that the nineteenth century slept and would not wake up. Nietzsche, despite the fact that he was a little, nervous man of great physical weakness, is yet far the most powerful force of his age. He seems anti-Christian, he was mistaken in his fundamental notion of the coming of the Superman, but his work is full of a new poetry. It is insisted that he was brutal in what he said about women. That is something personal in Nietzsche. Women wounded him. With his terrible physical suffering and his marvellous vision and passion he was in need of the love and faith of a real woman. But it was not his lot to find such a woman. He needed a harbour and an anchor, but it was his lot to toss ever on the shelterless sea.

Not a word is breathed against Nietzsche in Russia; too many lovers there have whispered the poetry of Zarathustra to one another. There is mistaken Nietzscheanism there, and talk of "all is permitted," but that is merely the vulgarisation of the age. Almost all the noble spirits of modern Russia have drunk deep of the wells of Nietzsche. As I said, the Nietzsche family sprang originally from Poland. He was really a Pole, a Slav— the German spirit is merely the dross in his writing. It is the Slavic that is the gold. As the great Russian tale-writer Kouprin writes in an open letter to Arthur Schnitzler: "Perhaps you think Nietzsche was one with you in your thoughts. No! Even we, your present enemies, could not gather in our souls so much hatred and contempt for you Prussians as Nietzsche poured forth in his works."

The true admirer of the Germans was our own Carlyle, whom Nietzsche cheerfully dismisses as "a muddlehead." Recent visitors to Ecclefechan, Carlyle's birthplace, will probably have seen the scarcely faded wreaths sent by the Kaiser to the memory of the Briton whom Germany honours most. Carlyle's belief in the Germans and in their ways was colossal. Did he not waste the ripeness of his life poring over the musty records of German military exploits? In the history of this war, and our re-estimate of the Germans we shall have to reconsider Carlyle and the "marching song of the Teutonic nations."

Maurice Maeterlinck's contribution to the question of the destiny of the Germans was one much considered in Russia, Maeterlinck holding an extremely high place in the esteem of the *intelligentsia*. It was translated at once into Russian and much commented upon. It was hailed with enthusiasm as giving a strong lead, and showing how the West had made up its mind to carry the war through to a terrible end. I must say I felt somewhat aghast at the hatred of Germany.

"They will say to us afterwards that the unfortunate German peoples were only the victims of their monarch and their system. That on the Germany we know, so cordial and so kind, no blame should fall—but only on Prussia—impatient, hateful, aggressive Prussia. The domestic, peace-loving Bavarians, the kind, hospitable dwellers on the shores of the Rhine, the Silesians, Saxons, and I know not who else will become at once as white as snow, less offending than the sheep on the pasture land.

"But now, whilst we stand face to face with reality, let us pronounce sentence : 'The German Empire must be destroyed as a wasps' nest. The Germans must be destroyed as we destroy a wasps' nest, since we know the wasps' nest can never become a bees' nest.'

" If eighty million innocent people support a monster-Kaiser, it shows simply the superficiality of their innocence and the inner falsehood of their nature. Should even a thousand years of civilisation pass in peace, the subconscious spirit of the Germans will still be as it is to-day. It will still be ready to show itself."

These are significant passages in the Russian version. Its tone is in strange contrast to the contribution of our J. M. Barrie, where the spirit of culture comforts the stricken Kaiser with the words: "If God is with the Allies, Germany will not be destroyed."

We British have a considerable amount of affection for our foe. The soldiers especially are on very good terms with the soldiers they are fighting—despite white flag incidents, bad German tricks, atrocities, cathedral-shelling, cutting out the eyes of the wounded and the like. There is a weakness towards Germany latent in our people, even an unfortunate weakness. When Germany is clearly beaten a great many people will raise their voice on her behalf. As yet, though, Germany has to be beaten.

Maeterlinck says, "Only from the depths of the most fearful and cruel injustice can we see what Justice is." That is an astonishingly wrong utterance, but it explains the fury of Maeterlinck's condemnation of the Germans, and it is a noble explanation. Maeterlinck is a Belgian.

How much more angry, how much more eager for German blood are the· Belgians and the French, those who have suffered, than we are! If the fortune of war goes rapidly against the foe, and Belgians and French get the Germans on the run, there is likely to be such revenge and plunder and ravaging that those in England who would spare Germany will find they have to witness the clearing off of a hate of which as yet they have but a sentimental notion. Iron has entered the souls of Belgian and French. The French have a long score to clear off, and they at least will not be inclined to make peace till Germany is in the dust, till they have exacted to the uttermost farthing and the last drop the treasure and blood exacted by the Germans in 1870. In weighing up the chances of the later stages of the war let us not under-estimate the driving power of French and Belgian hate. Later on we shall stand and watch the French taking vengeance. We do not perhaps hate sufficiently bitterly to do all that they will do.

The part which France is playing in this war and the part which she will play later on are being too little considered. But it is from France that Germany will receive her worst humiliation.

THE FUTURE OF THE POLES

A POLISH peasant woman and a Russian baba were talking in the train. "What dreadful things the Germans are doing!" says the Russian woman, a heavily clothed old wife who has come 1,000 versts by train in order to find and nurse her son who is seriously wounded. "What things they are doing to women, to the churches. They've ruined a great cathedral somewhere, I've read."

"Yes," says the Polish woman, "and our Pope has written against them."

"A new one isn't he, surely?"

"Yes, the old Pope died at the beginning of the war; it broke his heart."

"Trying to make peace among his children, eh? Clearly the Austrians are his, aren't they?"

"Yes, they are ours, too."

"Ah, how they oppress the poor Slavs, the Czechs, the Serbs, the others. Barbarians, that's what they are."

· "Yes, barbarians."

This word all the Russian peasants have got hold of. Ask the peasant what he thinks of the Germans. "Barbarians," he answers.

But it is an interesting opposition that of Pole and Austrian, both Roman Catholics. It is rather surprising that the Poles, extremely pious Roman Catholics as they are, have no particular sympathy with their co-religionists in Austria, and that the Pope throws the balance of his power rather into the scale against Germany and Austria. The fact is, Rome stands to gain more from the success of the Allies than from German domination.* German success means a stronger Protestant influence in the world generally—it means certainly a stronger influence in Austria; even the unification of the German and Austrian empires is possible. On the other hand, the success of Russia means, or ought to mean, I presume, the establishment of the Poles as a nation once more, though under the protection of the Tsar. What Rome has lost in France she can make up in autonomous Poland (and autonomous Ireland) when once the war has ended in the dispersal of the German dream of empire.

Poland, if restored, would be a great Roman Catholic country. Of that there can be no doubt. The Poles are a passionately national people. Nationalism is the biggest thing with them, and in their nationalism is included necessarily their religious faith. The Russians have tried in vain to Russify Poland; Poland remains crazily Polish. The Poles have emigrated to America in enormous numbers, but in America they do not tend to enter the choir dance of the races. They live together, as I have seen them in the mining villages of Pennsylvania, and have their political clubs, and talk their own old language, and read their own books, and write poems about Poland. They are a very poetical people; every third Pole writes verses. They are not in such numbers as the Irish in America, and since they are not English-speaking they have not the power of the Irish, but by virtue of their political organisation they are more like the Irish than other races.

* The Pope's only fear is of the Eastern Orthodox Church and its great increase in pomp and power that will follow the fall of Constantinople.

At the Cossack picnic: stirring the cauldron
of soup with birch branches.

Friendship of Russians and Poles

And despite the fact that Poles and Russians are equally Slavonic and are psychologically akin, yet how the Poles have hated the Russians! It would be impossible to hate more. The hate of brothers, when they do hate, is worse than the hate of those who are unrelated. It used to be almost equivalent to an insult to speak Russian in a Polish shop, or order your dinner in Russian at the restaurant. Now, however, things have changed.

I have just been staying in the fine old city of Vilna, a city of courtly Poles, the home of many of the old noble families of Poland. It is now thronged with Russian officers and soldiers. Along the main street is an incessant procession of troops, and as you look down you see vistas of bayonet spikes waving like reeds in a wind. As you lie in bed at night you listen to the tramp, tramp, tramp of soldiers. Or you look out at the window and see wagons and guns passing for twenty minutes on end, or you see prancing over the cobbles and the mud the Cossacks of the Don, of the Volga, of Seven Rivers. In the days of the revolutionary outburst the Poles bit their lips in hate at the sight of the Russian soldiers, they cursed under their breath, darted out with revolvers and shot, aimed bombs. To-day they smile, tears run down their cheeks; they even cheer. Whoever would have thought to see the day when the Poles would cheer the Russian troops marching through the streets of their own cities!

The Russians are forgiven. They come now to deliver the Slavs, not, as formerly, to trample on them. Go into a restaurant and order your dinner in Russian and you are smiled at and treated specially. To be a Russian is to be a *friend*. The Russians, also, with that

Russia and the World

complete turn-round of feeling of which the Slavonic peoples are so capable, are quite affectionate towards the Poles. It is said that since the proclamation of the Grand Duke Nicholas there has been quite a demand for Polish grammars and dictionaries on the part of Russians wishing to learn Polish. I, for my part, directly I read that proclamation, decided to learn some Polish, for I understood that Poland had suddenly begun to count.

A very touching spectacle may be seen every day just now at the Sacred Gate of Vilna. Above the gateway is a chapel with wide-open doors showing a richly gilded and flower-decked image of the Virgin. At one side stands a row of leaden organ pipes, at the other stands a priest. Music is wafted through the air with incense and the sound of prayers. Down below in the narrow, muddy roadway kneel many poor men and women with prayer books in their hands. They are Poles. But through the gateway come incessantly, all day and all \night, Russian troops going to the front. And as he approaches, every soldier, be he officer or private, lifts his hat and passes through the praying throng uncovered. This is beautiful. Let Russia always be so in the presence of the Mother of Poland.

No nation in modern history has been treated the way Poland has been treated, divided up like spoil and given to the three Emperors of Europe—living spoil. The history of Poland previous to partition is one of splendour and gallantry. A Dumas would have found in that history stories as gay and brave as in the history of France. The Poles were a bright and interesting contrast to their neighbours, the laborious Germans and the frozen Russians. They were an energetic, tireless people; they would have made out of Poland something distinctive.

The Messianic Nation

But Fate came across them. The wonderful nineteenth century came on and Poland was not. Poland was denied the opportunities of other Powers. England built up her mighty civilisation; Germany grew into form and was conscious of itself, and learned to speak with a strong, national voice; even Russia emerged out of the forests and the vast distances and built up a nineteenth-century civilisation. But Poland lay under the feet of conquerors.

To such a poignancy did Polish sorrow come, to such a degree of historical melancholy, that the Polish poets of the 'seventies came to write of Poland as the Messianic nation, the nation and the country that must be crucified and divided up, that must die and be buried. They formed a prophecy that through the sufferings of Poland the world would find regeneration. The Poles, many of them, learned to participate in a religious sorrow and find the accompanying religious consolation. Poland had to die that the world through Poland might be saved; Poland will rise again as a sign that every nationality has an immortality.

So now in this great struggle wherein the heavens are rent over the agony of Teutons and Slavs the Poles see a dove descending with the promise of peace. Poland is about to rise again.

The promises of poetry and religion seem more certain than the promises of politicians and of monarchs. If we turn from the melancholy beauty of this Polish idea to the sharp-edged actualities of politics, it is possible to feel that the restoration of the Polish nation is not so certain, that it is not so likely the providence of the Tsar will look God-dispensed as man-dispensed.

Russia and the World

I believe that if Germany is thoroughly beaten in the field, and granted not honourable but humiliating terms of peace, it will be possible to take German Poland from her, and from Austria Austrian Poland, though it means tearing them from the living flesh of Germany* and Austria respectively, and these may be added to Russian Poland and given a constitution under the protectorate of the Tsar. No new monarch is likely to be found for Poland, for the simple reason that monarchs of small States foment dissensions, and that the jealousy of the Courts of Servia, Bulgaria, Rumania, and Greece have caused so much trouble and misunderstanding that the Tsar is not likely to institute another Court. Collective Poland will probably be given a qualified home rule; she will have considerable control over her own finances and expenditure, the Polish language will become current at such universities as she may prefer to make peculiarly Polish, she will have power to organise the education of her people and to make herself a strong and loyal nation. What Mother Russia wants to see in Poland is an eldest son at her side.

Of course, when the war is over, and if the fabric of civilisation holds together, Russia has a great, a difficult task. It would be much easier to evade her obligations than to fulfil them. But she is not likely to evade them. There is every indication that she has entered on a new era as far as the government of Poland is concerned. Panslavism is going to progress positively by way of encouraging what is truly Slavonic, rather than negatively, as of old, by the repression of what was not Slavonic.

When once the war is over, Poland will be one of the

* German Poland takes in Dantzig and Posen and extends to within fifty miles of Berlin. Königsberg, however, does not belong to ancient Poland.

Roman Catholic Poland

most interesting countries in the world. All eyes will be turned on Russia to see how she will work out the great problem of giving Poland restitution. It is a problem that will task the genius of Russia, and test her patience and gentleness.

Just to touch on one or two of the difficulties, there is the jealousy of the Churches, of the ecclesiastics of the Churches. The Eastern Orthodox Church has very little in common with the Roman Catholic Church. It is indeed nearer to the Church of England than to Rome. But it will have to tolerate a fervently Roman Catholic Poland, and trust Polish nationalism to give Roman Catholicism what may be called an Eastern tinge or complexion.

The peasantry of Poland are most simple and pious. Of the Roman Catholics who arrive at Jerusalem on pilgrimage, some of the most humble and sincere are the Poles. There is a redeeming touch of mysticism in Polish religion. Though the Church accepts the responsibility for all dogma, and would relieve the lay person of discovering anything for himself, or of learning anything individually in his heart, yet by nature the Pole has visions, sees the mystic side of things, and has gleams of natural religion. Of course, the political influence of Rome will be greatly suspected by the Russian authorities. But everything is to be gained by trusting the Poles, rather than by mistrusting them.

The Government of Russia will fear that under the cover and protection of autonomy the Poles will be able to conspire effectively for complete independence. Conspiracy is congenial to the minds of the Poles—they have been great conspirators and plotters—though necessarily Polish plots have up to now, thanks to the vigilance of Russian police and the power of Russian armies, had very little success. It is difficult to believe that when the Poles have extra chances they will not work together for a complete national independence, for an army of their own, frontiers and tariff-barriers between them and Russia, foreign alliances and the rest. This fear may easily lessen the amount of freedom granted to Poland.

One stumbling-block is the mutual jealousies of the Churches, another is Polish ambition, a third that I may mention is the presence in Poland of almost all the Jews in the Russian Empire. There is no love lost between the Jews and the Poles. They have been fellow-sufferers and have merged their personal dislike of one another in their common hatred of the Russian autocracy. But that is all: the establishment of several million Jews in Poland has been one of the great difficulties of Poland. There are considerably more Jews than Russians in Poland —the country has rather been Judaised than Russianised. Jewry has given to Poland its characteristic complexion. In many districts the Jews outnumber the Poles.*

The Jews will hope to profit by Polish emancipation, and realise themselves as a nation in Poland. That is a danger. It would mean the continuous persecution of Poland by the Russians, who, as long as they remain Christian in the Byzantine sense, will always be in opposition to Judaism and that materialism for which in their eyes Judaism stands. Jewry must keep only a second or third place in Poland. To the establishment of that end greater facilities for emigration to the United States will probably be afforded the Jews. There the Jews are greatly in the ascendant, and are indeed realising themselves as a nation as never before. Western Christianity, with its

---

* Historically the Poles are responsible for the Jews. They invited the Jews to settle in Poland in the Middle Ages.

Reconstitution of Poland

insistence on ethics rather than on religious sense, finds nothing incompatible in Judaism. America is for Russian Jews, as Mary Antin pointed out, the true promised land.

The Jews, with that sweet reasonableness, kindness, and common sense which distinguish their life when they are not too embittered by persecution, will perhaps see that no good end is served by fanning malice against Russia, and they will turn their eyes rather towards the West than towards the East. So Poland will escape Jewish predomination, and also political deprivations on account of Jewish conditions.

But this statement of the case is all on the assumption that German and Austrian Poland will be added to Russian Poland. We leave out of account the possibility that Germany may not be so utterly beaten that she will be forced to part with a great stretch of thoroughly Germanised territory. If the war leaves the old Eastern frontier line untouched, Russia will not feel that she is in a position to resurrect Poland. For she would only have charge of a third of the old Polish land. One thing, however, is certain, even under these conditions, and that is Polish and Russian friendship. Russia will do what she can for her Polish subjects. As we all hope for complete victory in the strife, so we look beyond the struggle to one of the first fruits of peace, the reconstitution of the ancient land of Poland, the sewing together of the mantle that the Emperors divided between them.

For the time being, however, the hurly-burly rages. The Russians are noble in war, and Poland waits, gently hoping, and fearing also, like a woman who is to be married if her soldier comes home safe from the war.

THE FUTURE OF THE JEWS

RUSSIA'S great instinctive struggle is against Westernism. She has a great treasure in her national life, but
she does not know how she came by it and does not know
how to keep it. But she continually notices how she is
losing that treasure, how it tends to slip away from her,
and she makes great clumsy efforts to save herself and it.
Hence much that is unnecessarily barbarous, much that is
unjust and even stupid in the regime of Russia. Hence,
for instance, the great ritual murder trial at Kief. Nothing
could have been more clumsy and impolitic than this trial,
and from a Western point of view nothing more unjust
than its intention. The prosecution was an act of hostility
against the Jews in Russia, an attempt to hasten the exodus
of the Jews to America, and to put in a worse position those
who remained behind. For the Russian patriot cannot
tolerate the Jew—he sees in him the whole instinct of
materialism and Westernism and commercialism.

The Jews, especially in their new awakening, are a
Western nation. They find their natural home in America.
Zionism, despite the sincerity of Jewish Zionists, is a sen-
timentalism with many Jews, bluff with others. The
Jews can never settle in great numbers in Palestine. But
in America they already tend to be a dominant factor in the
population of that country. Our blood-relationship with
the Americans, it may be said in passing, is something
decidedly on the wane. The Jews to-day are on the up-

grade. They are not being persecuted so much as of yore; indeed, on the contrary, as employers of labour they begin themselves to persecute others. Be that as it may, they are availing themselves of all the opportunities of civilisation, and going forward to be masters. They are not so earnest in their religious rites, not so exclusive of the Gentile, inclined to marry into Christian families—even in Russia they are accepting baptism in considerable numbers. All good Russians must wish the Jews Godspeed when they see them embarking for America at Libau, not because they are an evil people or accursed, but because with their genius and their assumed humility they have ever been a great danger to the Russians. It is a truism to say that if the revolution succeeded, or if freedom were granted to all the peoples, the Jews would overrun Russia, and all the secular power would fall into their hands.

As Christians denying the world it is difficult to see on what ground Russians trouble themselves so much about worldly conditions. They are positively afraid of the Jews.

One said to me: "How your country is falling into the hands of the Jews: your Lord Chief Justice is a Jew."

"Isn't it splendid," said I, "the head of the Law is a Jew. Now, if a Jew had been appointed Archbishop of Canterbury we might have had cause to complain."

What has a true Christian got to do with law? When he goes to law, he ceases for the time being to be a Christian from the Eastern or Byzantine point of view. Now, the Jews understand law and the judgment by a code, and law is one of the professions best suited to their temperament. The Jews are good lawyers, good bankers, brokers, commercial travellers, shipping agents, chess-players, mathematicians, and also good musicians. The weak spot in their materialistic armour is music. Through music they find access sometimes to the things of the spirit. We should not feel their success at law—like goes to like.

"A scandal, however," said my friend. "What justice can there be between Jews and Christians? Their Talmud tells them that any means against the Christian are justifiable"—and so on, the whole anti-Semitic diatribe now stale by repetition.

But to revert to the case of the ritual murder trial. A Christian boy had been found done to death in a horrible fashion, his veins cut in a special way with knives, forty wounds in his body—the position of the wounds having evidently some sort of mystic significance. Beiliss was innocent; but someone was guilty, a madman or a Jew, and indeed the probability is that a Jew did actually commit the crime. Whether it was for ritual purposes or not is another matter.

Most people would agree that it was a great mistake on the part of the Russian Government to fight the Jews on the count of the murder of a Christian child. If among the illiterate and savage Jews that dwell in the remoter parts of the Pale there should exist dark sects in whose rites child-sacrifice, Moloch worship, and the like are practised, it is merely a curiosity among religions of contemporary Europe. But the great quarrel of Russians with Jews is not on that ground. They would willingly spare the Jews an accidental Christian child now and then. No, it is with the Jewish business spirit and Jewish enmity towards Christianity and towards the "unprofitable" Christian life, that the Russian has his quarrel.

The main result of the trial was that it brought the question of anti-Semitism to the touchstone of common sense. Up till now Jews have been hated or protected

emotionally, but throughout the world there has naturally
set in an intellectual inquiry into the merits or demerits
of the anti-Semitic case. The most significant thing about
the Beiliss trial was that the Jewish people had the power
to obtain from a court set on injustice the verdict of "Not
guilty." It proved that for the time being the argument
of physical force was not available against the Jews. It
turned the question into the channels of the Press, the
pamphlet, the ordinary conversation. Henceforth there
was much less chance of pogroms.

Russia has to decide why she hates the Jews. Obviously
she does not hate them because they occasionally murder
a Christian child—that is an absurdly Western reason, even
if the fact were true—that is only the red flag of the
massacre, the pretext, the inevitable lie in whose name
murder is committed. There is something much deeper
in this great national animosity, something which logic
and common sense cannot get over.

There are two parties in Russia; a large one that
distrusts the Jew and believes evil of him, a small one
which protects him. But as regards "ritual murder" it is,
of course, a comparatively small number that believes the
Jews are guilty of the practice.

One of the most interesting phenomena of the time
has been the persecution of the brilliant anti-Semitic
pamphleteer Rozanof, one of the contributors of the *Novoe
Vremya*, and a writer recognised by every one as being in
the foremost rank in Russia. His primary feeling about
the Jews may be summarised from a book of his con-
fessions, "Fallen Leaves."

"The Jew always begins with service and serviceableness and ends
with power and mastership. In the first stage he is difficult to grapple
with. What are you to do with a man who simply stands and puts

himself at your service? But in the second stage no one can get equal with him. Countries and nations perish—

"The services of the Jews are like nails in my hands, the 'caressingness' of the Jews burns me like a flame. For profiting by the one my nation perishes, and blown upon by the other my nation rots and dies. We are all running to the Jews for help. And in a hundred years all will be *with the Jews*."

This was written long before the Beiliss case. During the trial Rozanof came forward and contributed to the *Novoe Vremya* and other papers a most substantial account of the ritual practices of the Jews. Credit must be given him for extraordinary research. He had gone into the depths of black magic as propounded in almost inaccessible volumes on occultism, and had come back with a circumstantial case against secret sects of the Jews. He explained the hieroglyphics of the wounds of Yushinsky. He insisted that the great agitation made by the Jews was due to their fear that their secrets were about to be unveiled, and bringing a wide culture and incisive journalistic wit to bear on the subject he certainly convinced many who wished to be convinced, and, on the other hand, set a most influential band of Russian writers and thinkers against him.

Merezhkovsky and Struvé and several other members of the Religious and Philosophical Society of St. Petersburg, one of the most important literary societies in Russia, protested against the membership of Rozanof, making a motion to expel him, enforcing the motion by threatening to withdraw themselves if he were still allowed to be a member. They could not continue to work with a man who held such opinions. The motion was defeated, but Rozanof on his own account resigned. Jew-lovers are also ready to persecute; pro-Semitism has its victims, as

The Real Reason of Dislike

well as anti-Semitism. Rozanof has lately collected his articles into a book, "The Relation of the Jews to Blood," and several Liberal newspapers have refused advertisements of it. It is a very powerful, interesting, and curious volume. It is rather difficult for a Russian to read it without being shaken. But then the practice of drinking blood and the existence of secret rites is a commonplace to the Russian, and his mind is prepared for a serious consideration of ideas which in the West have no countenance. The Jews have never been found sacrificing Christian children in England or America, and that necessarily binds the Anglo-Saxon race in the belief that ritual murder is a myth.

The question remains: Why are the Russians so antagonistic to the Jews? All Russians know a Jew at once by his face and his manners, so intense is the dislike of the type. There is something more in it than the arguments of this curious *cause célèbre*. I think it is due to the fundamental opposition of the Jewish character to that which is most precious in the Slav. The Tartar in the Russian is a similar type to the Jew—and indeed many hold that the Russian Jews are not Hebraic, but simply the descendants of Tartar converts to Judaism. The Tartar gets on happily with the Jew, but the fundamentally Slavonic, the mystical, the careless, that part of the soul of the Russians which makes them like the Celts in temperament, cannot agree with the Jew. To him the Jew is poison. Russia considers its Tartar nature the lower nature. All love of Russia and pride in Russia is love of the other and pride in the other. All that is precious in Russian life, art, literature, music, religion, springs from the other—the gay carelessness, the despising of material possessions, the love of the neighbour, the mystical.

Russia and the World

The Jews, with their grasp of trade, their sympathy
with Westernism and contempt of mysticism, endanger
the Russian ideal. They have great power in the
Press; the Russian Government therefore keeps a strict
censorship over the Press, flinging editors into prison
right and left, confiscating numbers of journals, inflicting
huge fines. The Jews are strongly entrenched in the
legal profession, and are credited with making immense fortunes by dubious means—and Russians revenge themselves
weakly by exacting heavy blackmail when they can. The
Jews in the secret police bought and sold the revolution; witness the cases of Azef* and Bogrof. The Jews
are the main manipulators of emigration to America
and elsewhere, having a regular business of procuring
passengers for the transatlantic shipping companies, conducting the passportless across the Russian frontier, ob-
taining premiums from South American trust companies
for providing gangs of workers. They are too clever for
the Russians, or Russians are too easily corrupted. The
consequence is, that no broad legal measure is ever carried out in such a way as to stop the practices. The
result of this Russian impotency is irritation and petulancy
on the part of the clean-handed, and inflamed malice on
the part of the bribe-takers. Because of this, which cannot be tracked down and settled between the Jew and
the Russian, the latter has recourse to wanton massacre,
to trial for ritual murder and the like. The proscription
of Rozanof marked an interesting development in this
hostility. Liberal Russia will perhaps make up her mind
to protect the Hebrews, and the Duma of the future will
perhaps free them and put in their hands what is their

* Azef, a Russian Jew, who arranged, among other murders, the assassination of
the Grand Duke Serge, was both a member of the secret police and a leader in the
revolutionary party.

British Sympathy with the Jews

due—business and the law. But how will the Church and the aristocracy and the poor religious mystical peasant put a bridle on the power that money and the law would eventually give the Jew in idle Russia?

The war raises the question of the rights of Jewry in another form. It has come about that the Russian and British Governments are in alliance. The Jews have been working against the possibility of such an alliance for many years. They have used every opportunity to cultivate in the British and American peoples an abhorrence of Russian Government. But behold, thanks to Germany's hate of England and the maturing of that hate to war, we are all friendly towards Russia. The campaign of the Jews and those whom they had converted to hatred of Russia is badly left. If it could have been possible for England to remain neutral in this conflict, there would undoubtedly have been a great campaign of defamation of Russia.

England, however, has great sympathy with the Jews. If the Russian authorities allow massacres, or if such mistaken prosecutions are insisted on as that of Beiliss, England will be cold towards Russia and Russia will feel her coldness. Russia should know this.

The great question is: Is Russia going to do anything for the Jews when the war is over? Many think that Russia has promised emancipation, but, of course, she has not. The Jews are conducting a very effective propaganda in the Press, watching, criticising, correcting all the statements made about the Jews by journalists and authors. Unfortunately, of those who write about Russia very few have any clear idea either of Russia herself or of the Jewish Pale; they either depict unrelieved horror, or they talk of their personal dislike of the Jewish type,

Russia and the World

Jewish ways, Jewish clothes and so on. Consequently, the correcting of journalism is a very useful way of propagandising.

The Jewish difficulty is that the Poles have been promised something as Poles, but the Jews have been promised nothing. The Belgians, the French and the British promise themselves certain rewards on the day of victory, but the Jews as Jews have been promised nothing at all, and cannot promise themselves anything. Jewry has made up its mind that though it has not been promised anything, it intends to get something out of it all.

With that end in view the Jews lay emphasis on the loyalty of Jews and on the exploits of Jewish soldiers. They are entitled to do so. There are thousands of Jews fighting in the English, French and Belgian armies, not, of course, as Jews, but as British, French or Belgian subjects respectively. There are tens of thousands serving in the Russian army. There they are serving as Jews rather than as Russians—for a Jew is denied many privileges of Russian nationality. But of course the Jew is compelled to serve—he has no say in the matter.

An English correspondent writes to me that we must remember that the Russian Jews could have remained neutral if they had chosen. This shows the sort of notion that gets abroad through partisan propaganda. The Jews had no choice in the matter. They might have rebelled and so been shot down under martial law—in that sense only had they a choice.

The pro-Jewish propaganda insists on the heroism of Osnas, whom the Tsar decorated, and on the valorous deeds of the Jews serving in the Russian army. They point to the suffering and death of many Jewish soldiers,

The Jewish Claim

and also to the privations of Jewish families in the districts ravaged by the Germans, and they say: Does all this go for naught? Every true Englishman's answer is, It ought not to go for naught; the Jews should be shown exceptional kindness when the war is over.

But there is another side of the argument which is not indicated in the propaganda. It is that there are also thousands of German Jews fighting in the German army, and fighting as well, suffering as much. There is also a great number of Jews in England and America who in season and out of season pursue a propaganda against Russia, chilling the friendly spirit which at present exists between Russia and the other Allies. The Russians have been staunch and loyal friends of the English and French, and have withstood all manner of seductive proposals made to them by the Germans with the object of detaching them. The Jews cannot at present claim that they are helping our cause very much. Still, that is no reason why the Jews should be done injustice or rendered liable to further persecution in Poland. It is to be hoped that within the Jewish Pale they will be granted certain privileges of education and emigration, and that they be better safeguarded from the individual malice of Jew-baiters.

The question of what Russia is going to do for the Jews was put to me lately by one of our most distinguished British Jews, the Lord Chief Justice. I give the conversation. Imagine the glittering, clear-cut features of one who has been eminent in law, politics, and finance. I found myself sitting next to him one night at dinner.

We talked of Russia, of the optimism which prevails in Russia, of the prospects of Poland's autonomy, and

143

then at last . . . "There is one question I should like to ask you specially," said my neighbour, "that is, what do you think is likely to be the position of the Jews at the end of the war? Do you think anything will be done for them?"

"Not very much," I answered. "They will not obtain freedom to go where they wish in the Russian Empire. The Russian Church without wavering is against the Jews, and, as you know, the Court itself not only has no tolerance for the Jews, but is ready to believe anything against them, anything like the ritual murder, for instance. One thing I gather from my conversation with Sazonof: they are likely to be excused military service."

"As a privilege?" he asked.

"Yes, of course as a privilege, not as a new deprivation. The Jews are strongly against military service."

Then the conversation dropped for a few minutes, to be taken up later.

I turned to my neighbour and asked:

"Is the Government likely to ask for special clauses in the treaty of peace safeguarding Russia's treatment of the Jews?"

"We shall not have to conclude peace with Russia, who is our ally, but with Germany," was the answer.

"But the Jews are making a great deal of propaganda just now. They are showing a great deal of distrust of Russia, and they evidently intend raising the question in a very formidable fashion when once peace is in sight."

"I think perhaps America may put forward some proposition."

"What do you think can be done?" I asked. "The Jews cannot realise themselves as a nation in Christian

A Way Out for the Jews

Russia; they don't seem very much pleased with what I wrote in *The Times* about their realising themselves as a nation in America. Have you any personal belief in Zionism?"

He did not seem to think it likely that the Children would return to Palestine.

Nevertheless, the air just now is full of prophecy about the return of the Jews. The Jews themselves are whispering much about the fulfilment of the old prophecies, and though it is not likely that the Rothschilds and the great financiers will go to Jerusalem, I believe there may be something in the possibility of the re-establishment of the Jews in Palestine as a nation.

One of the possibilities of the war is the fall of the Turkish Empire and the liberation of Syria from the Mohammedan yoke. Palestine becomes vacant, or at least eligible for a new Government. It seems to me that something might be done for the establishment of the Jews in Palestine.

The Jews won't go there all at once. That is evident. But a Jewish Government might be formed there of financiers and representative Jews. Once a Government has been formed, it could be made optional for the Jews to give up their various European national papers and become Jewish subjects. Russian Jews could then cease to be Russian subjects and become Jewish subjects; German Jews could become Jewish subjects, and so on. They would have the financial and moral protection of their own Government. They could in time form a democracy in Palestine if they wished it; they could have their own army and navy if necessary.

This would be a great blessing to the world. Already the chief reason that the Russian peasant has for calling the Jew accursed is that he has no land of his own. For instance, when the Russians were retreating in Poland I asked a common soldier the reason. His answer was—"The Jews betray us. That's what comes of having an accursed people *without any land of their own;* they dog our steps and sell us at every turn. If we are winning they come round us and praise us, and try to help us; if we begin to lose they run to the enemy and say, 'Don't you ill-treat us; we are your friends; we can help you; we have valuable information.'" The Jews ought to have a place of their own and a Government of their own. They ought not to be always fighting for their separate interests in the life of foreign nations.* They are a great people, and are now, as never before, on the upgrade in civilisation. They ought to be officially united. The world of Gentiles also is interested to see them as a nation, and would welcome any steps the Jews might take towards the realisation of themselves as such.

The brevities of the Jewish situation may be stated thus:

(i) Russia has promised little to the Jews and will give little.

(ii) England has sympathy with the Jews.

(iii) America will help the Jews if she can.

(iv) The Jews are working hard for themselves.

(v) I suggest that if the Turkish Empire falls, a Jewish Government should be established in Palestine, and Jews all the world over should have the option of becoming Jewish subjects.

* Even in England, where on the whole we like the Jews, there are many who are Jew first and English only second. The English Jews campaigning against Russia, with whom we are in alliance, are obviously more Jew than English, and are candidates for Palestine.

TURKS

THE covetousness of Turkey has overcome fear of consequences, and her perennial enmity has matured once more to war. Behold, in addition to the wild strife of Europe, another Turkish war. Belgium has been overrun and ruined, Poland has been overrun, and the Caucasus and Crimea are to have equal ruin with these unfortunate countries—massacre, devastation, robbery. Not only the Caucasus and Crimea, but also Syria and Palestine, where are large colonies of Russians and English, and many French and Belgians with commercial interests. The wealth of Beirut, Smyrna and Jaffa is to a great extent European wealth. The powerful Russian settlement in Jerusalem is in danger, and also the lives of the gentle and cultured British who are attached to the English mission.

The war is a continuous calamity for non-combatants —a campaign of organised plunder and loot. It will hardly be Turkey's policy to fight pitched battles, and so be beaten in the field. She will rather avoid the Russian troops, seek out unprotected districts, and make inroads. The great Russian army mobilised in Transcaucasia is bound to have victories, but they will not cause ultimate anxiety to the Turks; the natural difficulties in the way of conquering Asia Minor are almost insuperable. A small force of irregulars and Turkish brigands could keep a great army employed for a long time.

Russia and the World

The native Turkish population is very hostile and warlike, and there is the prospect of protracted guerilla warfare. I do not see Russia getting to Constantinople by way of these mountains and deserts. It's a long, long way. The first phase of the Russian-Turkish conflict depends on the success or failure of the Black Sea Fleet. If the Turks and Germans sink the Russian warships, such as they are, they can choose what points they like on the long line of seashore, and bring up their barbarous troops and make inroads and pillage. Many such inroads have already been made—to judge from private correspondence I have seen—but the Russian Censor suppresses all details. But if the Russian fleet disposes of the Turkish and German warships, Russia can land troops much nearer to Constantinople and the heart of Turkey. Unfortunately, owing to the security of the Bosphorus, the Turks have a retiring-place as good as the Kiel Canal in the other theatre of war. If the Turkish fleet is cautious it can prolong the struggle indefinitely.

Should the Turks obtain ascendancy in the Black Sea, the chief towns to suffer would be Odessa, Batum, Novorossisk, Poti, and Theodosia. The town of Sebastopol is probably impregnable ; Kherson and Nikolaief are somewhat difficult of access. The ports of the Azof Sea, the most important of which is Rostof-on-the-Don, have been saved by the shallowness of the sea and the early date of freezing. Rostof is the railway key of the Caucasus and a wealthy and important place.

All has changed since the days of the Crimean War. The Black Sea offers many targets, and Russia is much more vulnerable here. I have walked almost the whole of the Black Sea shore, from Sebastopol to Batum, a thousand miles and more, and so know it with unusual

The Black Sea Shore

intimacy. It is poor country, but there are many prizes for pirates. There is a whole chain of watering-places; there is the Tsar's favourite estate of Livadia, where the happiest hours of the Tsarevitch have been spent; there is Yalta, the favourite winter haunt of the aristocracy; there is the great monastery of New Athos, destroyed by the Turks in 1870, but built again over the ruins of the old building, and now one of the greatest institutions of its kind; there is wonderful little Gagri, with its rich villas, all ready to the hand of the spoiler, like bunches of wild grapes. There are no fortifications, no soldiers. Already even the inhabitants of the seashore villages have fled; the Turkish knife is known and feared.

It is not only the Turks who are feared, but the Mohammedan tribesmen of the Caucasus, very dangerous people even in time of peace; the Abkhastsi, the Mohammedan Ossetini, the Ingooshi, and a score more races, all armed and prone to murder and brigandage. The whole coast from Gagri to beyond Batum is necessarily sympathetic to the enemy. And in the interior of the Caucasus and in Transcaucasia there are bound to be risings. Russia will either have to allow her territory to fall under terrible ravage, or send a great quantity of troops to guard the various vital points of the shore. Tuapse, for instance, the oil port of Maikop, is now an important point, since the railway runs thither from Armavir through somewhat disaffected country. At Batum, Theodosia, Novorossisk, Sebastopol, and Odessa, distinct railway lines from Russia terminate; these are most important. There is as yet no coast railway.

But we wait for the success of the Russian Black Sea Fleet. The best vessels are the *Johann Zlato-Ust* and the *Efstafiy*, both built in 1906, and having a displacement

Russia and the World

of 13,000 tons. Then follows the *Pantalemon*, built 1900, and the *Rostislaf*, built 1896, and after these a tail of old and little vessels. Against this force sails the even more miserable Turkish fleet, whose best vessels are the *Barbarossa Haireden* and the *Forgud Reis*, both built in Germany in 1891, and displacing 10,060 tons. But Turkey has also the German light cruiser *Breslau* and the great, powerful modern Dreadnought *Goeben*, of 23,000 tonnage and 28 knots speed. If the modern warship is as superior in power as experts hold, then the *Goeben* should itself be able to sink the whole Russian Black Sea Fleet. The calamities of that vessel, however, lead one to hope that it has considerable defects or is inefficiently manned. Twice it has been forced back to Constantinople for repairs. It is now at large, and it recently shelled Batum. But it is steaming at a greatly reduced speed, owing to bad Turkish coal. It seems very possible that the bad luck that has attended its adventures in the Black Sea will continue, and that once more it will be disabled, and this time finally.

Many have asked, Why did not Russia declare war on Turkey and fall upon her in the midst of her preparations? But Russia, having her hands full with Austria and Germany, would rather not solve the problem of Turkey at present, much as she would like a crusade against the Saracen under ordinary conditions. The presence of two modern German warships in the Turkish fleet greatly increases the difficulty. Russia, thanks to her treaty obligations with Turkey, has never been able to bring any warships through the Dardanelles and the Bosphorus into the Black Sea, otherwise she would not be to-day in the position of a third-rate naval Power there. Probably the *Goeben* is the first great modern warship that has yet dipped into the waters of the

Popularity of the Turk

Euxine. Turkey has not even permitted guns to be taken through the Straits, and every vessel passing from Russia to the Ægean or back again has had to submit to being searched at the northern or southern entrance to the narrow waters. As long as the *Goeben* and the *Breslau* are on the sea, the Russians are obliged to keep great numbers of soldiers waiting at the points of possible invasion. It is worth Germany's while to keep Turkey fighting. Turkey's quarrel is worth 200,000 Russians less on the fields of Poland.

One of the surprises of the war has been that Turkey has been ready to squander our friendship. The Turks, as a people, have a great deal of respect and admiration for the British people. They regard us as their traditional friends. They are proud of the bits of English they know, and the sailors and dock labourers of Constantinople and Smyrna have even adopted some English into their speech, and you may frequently hear such expressions as "All right" and "Go-ahead" if you listen in the harbours. And the English have an esteem for the Turks. Many of our dear pagan fellow-countrymen down in the City have a soft spot in their hearts for the Turk. This was abundantly apparent at the time of the first Balkan War, when London was at the outset almost entirely in sympathy with Turkey. Of course, the Turks are very picturesque, rather simple in their national ways, and they observe the rites of their religion in good taste. They have the manners of gentlemen—some of them. But then there is everything in the Turkish Empire—Caucasian brigands, Bashi-Bazouks, Dervishes, Arabs. One rather wonders how Pierre Loti, with his great sentimental attachment to Turkey, views the present conflict. How will he view the split up of the Empire and the Christianising of so many parts of it?

If Russia beats Turkey thoroughly there should be little trouble in pacifying the Holy Land; if she takes Constantinople the Turkish Empire will be likely to fall to bits. That will be some consolation for the extra trouble to which the Allies have been put. Russia will hold a protectorate over Armenia, Constantinople and the access to the Mediterranean. Syria and Palestine may receive some measure of independence.

The Turkish hold on Syria is very light. Only about one-fifth of the population is Mohammedan; the remaining four-fifths is quite out of sympathy with Turkish rule, and would much rather govern itself or entrust its destinies to the French or English.

What will become of Palestine is rather an interesting problem. We hear little of Syrian home politics, and yet there is a strong national sentiment among Syrians the world over. If Syria were re-established as a State, a great number of rich Syrians would return to their native land—especially from America. The Syrians are mostly Christians, though they are Eastern in habits and keep their wives and domestic life much veiled.

Stronger claimants to rights in Palestine are the Jews. Ancient prophecy, the approval of the Gentile world and contemporary Jewish sentiment are all in favour of the re-establishment of the Jews in Syria. Zionism promises to settle the problem of the treatment of the Jews in the various countries of the world. If the peace that follows this war is founded on the principle that each nationality is entitled to govern itself on its own representative land, then it will be a case of Poland to the Poles, Alsace to the French, Ireland to the Irish, Jerusalem to the Jews, and so on.

The Fate of Jerusalem

There are, however, great difficulties. Jerusalem is a great Christian See. The Roman Catholics, the Orthodox Greeks and the Orthodox Russians, the Armenians, the Copts, all regard Jerusalem as a place made holy not so much by the Old, but by the New Testament, not by Jewish history, but by the holiest events in the founding of Christianity. The old wall where the Jews beat their heads on the stones and wail is not the holiest shrine in Jerusalem, but rather the sepulchre of Jesus; not the promise that there the Jews shall be gathered together again, but the symbolic fact of the life of the first great Pilgrim. Russian peasants, for instance, would be very averse from the idea of Bethlehem and Calvary belonging to the Jews.

Still, I suppose, whatever happens, the pilgrimaging to Jerusalem will be resumed by the Russian peasants when the war is over and the Straits are open again. Whatever happens, the same sweet pastoral life of Syrian shepherdesses and Bedouin Arabs with their tents will still go on. The Syrians are, of course, Turkish conscripts, but so many of them have deserted that the nation is more like a nation of non-combatants. The Russians have been arrested. Many monks and priests have been molested. There has been a considerable amount of pillaging of Christian shrines. The Greeks have to manage everything, but they are looked upon with hostility. There are continual alarms of massacre and outrage and many insurrectionary Arab gatherings. The Christian solemnisation of the baptism at Jordan and of Easter at Jerusalem will be without the chorus of pilgrim praise and the curious gaze of the tourist. The first Easter after the war should be a wonderful time.

AMERICANS

FEELING in America is now a great deal more pro-British than it was at the beginning of the war. But the fact that it was confessedly anti-British at the commencement of the war should make us very wary in our judgment. Anglo-American sentiment though showy is none the less sincere. We can accept it heartily. But it is a mistake to fix our eyes on it to the exclusion of other things in America. It is put in the foreground by American and British journalists, but from one point of view that is a mistake. It is much more important that we keep our eyes on the hostility that exists in the United States, and that we gauge its power. A number of Anglo-Americans are in the habit of thinking and talking and writing slightingly of Britain. Most of the German and Dutch Americans sympathise with the Germans; and the Jews, of whom there are 1,000,000 in New York alone, are, on the whole, pro-German, and are certainly anti-Russian. We are too much in the habit of assuming that America is peopled by British people who merely live under a President of their own instead of under our King. We forget the flow of foreign immigration into the States; we forget the trusts, the undue influence of money, the corruption in the administration. American reality is not our reality. American ideals are not our ideals. I hope America will not be called upon to interfere in the struggle, either as a belligerent or as a peace-maker. But in case it should happen that America comes in, it would be well for the British to keep a true picture of America and American ideals before them.

First of all, America is a commercial country. Business is her chief function. She has no landed gentry, no old peasant life with peasant customs.

America believes in universal peace. She sees no reason for such an unprofitable thing as war. She, for her part, desires to keep out of warfare. She has to that end made many arbitration treaties with other nations, and she thinks that she has at least removed the danger of being attacked. All the same, up to the outbreak of this great European War she lived in a certain amount of dread of a war with Germany, and many of her citizens, as, for instance, the late Price Collier, held that, with time, such a war was even probable. America as a pure democracy would vote against war every time. The power of government is not, however, in the hands of the democracy. Financiers have the power to sway the councils of the Government to their private ends, and so little wars are still possible. A war against Mexico, or against Spain, or some other third-rate Power is always a possibility, and though it is against the American ideal it would be tolerated, inasmuch as America stands to lose little by such a course. But a war with Japan, though possible and even probable from some points of view, would cause a great outcry in the States. For the Americans believe in universal peace.

America believes in health and success and prosperity. "America has no use for a sick man"—to quote a common saying. She has little sympathy with failure. What is beauty in the life of the Old World means nothing to

her. She admires ruins and curiosities and curios, but
in the spirit of the collector. She has a contempt,
born of ignorance, for ranks, for ceremonies, rituals,
liturgies. For her, Russian, German, Norwegian, Englishman, Frenchman, are, except for a difference in
language which can be overcome, one and the same.
They are, roughly speaking, of the same capabilities. If
she recognises differences in national individuality or
personal individuality, she does not love the differences,
does not prize the differences. Her own notions of
success and goodness she deems to be the only notions,
her own justice and fairness to be the only criterion of
justice and fairness. The characteristics of her own
destiny must, she thinks, show the characteristics of the
destiny of other countries. If other countries are not
like her they are simply backward.

Though there is a great deal of Liberal sentiment in
America, the Americans are not Liberal. In "Changing
Russia," I defined Liberalism as "Nationalism as opposed
to Imperialism; respect for the rights of individuals as
opposed to Collectivism; a belief in little nations rather
than in large empires. Liberalism encourages national
characteristics, distinctive language, dress, custom, the
barriers which keep people apart." America, by the
very fact of its conglomerative formation, is opposed to
these national characteristics, has a contempt for these
characteristics. She cannot, therefore, bring much light
to the settlement of the European struggle on the
desired Liberal and national lines of recognition of the
rights of small peoples not to be Prussianised or Russianised or Anglified. America's quite natural desire is to
Americanise everyone who comes to her. Her unfortunate
habit is to Americanise everything she touches.

THE GREAT WHITE TSAR

THE cannon speak louder than the voices of men in this war. Never were men so thrown into insignificance; never was there such a disparity between men and guns. Battles are won by guns rather than by men. It often seems as if the *issimus* tacked on to the word "general" were a diminutive, not a superlative, and that Generalissimus Joffre must be some sort of wonderful little ivory model or toy and not a man. We have only to read one of our fine old war-dramas, such as "Richard III.," to realise how much more did personal character and nobility count in the old days than now. When the history of this vast war is written, it will be almost impossible to take the personal history of some individual man and say, "There, in one man's life and passion lies the whole story of this European strife." The only figure that does stand out at present is that of the Kaiser, and possibly a Shakespeare of our age would find in the Kaiser's story the epic of the war. Unfortunately, we dislike the Kaiser too much to consider him calmly as Milton did Satan, or Shakespeare Richard III. It will be years before we can regard the Kaiser with clear eyes. But, meanwhile, there is one other figure in this war that stands out on the popular vision very remarkably, and that is the Tsar Nicholas II., once called the Great White Tsar.

When the Tsar came to the throne he showed

himself to be an idealist, even a Utopian idealist, by his passionate efforts for the establishment of universal peace. The cause of peace was chiefly associated with the name of the Tsar. It was strange that this great absolute monarch should associate himself with the cause dearest of all to democrats and Liberals, strange that he should be the colleague of men like W. T. Stead and Andrew Carnegie. Many said that the Tsar was not sincere. The sarcastic and cynical found Nicholas delivered wholly to their untender mercy when at last, owing to non-acceptance of Japanese demands, war broke out between Russia and Japan. But a worse denial of ideals was to follow when the great revolutionary outburst was put down ruthlessly by military force. The Tsar became "the man of blood." People associated the ghastly carnage of the war with the dreadful loss of life at the Coronation crush in Moscow, and with the firing on the workmen of Father Gapon's procession, and with many another incident in which the Tsar's name was connected with the injury and death of his subjects. Perhaps no one has been more hated in his time than the Tsar. No one has been more cursed.

And yet despite all that seemed against him, many people quietly kept their faith in him. The most touching example is perhaps that of W. T. Stead. Stead and many others saw in the Tsar the granter of the Duma, a new Peter the Great, a God-chosen monarch leading his nation through the most difficult and hazardous ways of national evolution. They held that it was comparatively easy for Alexander II. to give liberty to the serfs, but that it needed a stupendous genius to cope with the difficulties that that liberation would lead to. It must

Revolutionaries' Opinion of the Tsar

always be remembered that no Russian monarch previous to Nicholas II. has had to face 100,000,000 free peasants and working men. It must always have been said of him, even if he had been stricken in the revolution, that he was confronted by problems that only genius or sacred simplicity could solve.

He survived his passion for peace, his unfortunate war with Japan, his wild and bloody revolutionary era—to be laughed at. Attention was drawn to the fact that tens of thousands of soldiers lined the railway track whenever he made a journey to a city in his dominion, and that he dare not stir from his palace without an army to guard him, that before he went to the third city of the Empire he had several thousand people arrested as suspicious characters, that in many parts of Russia he dare not show himself even with these precautions. The precautions did cause one to pause and reflect, and yet we remember how at Kief the Jewish police agent Bogrof managed to get into the theatre in spite of all care, and only at the last moment changed his mind and shot Stolypin instead of His Majesty. The precautions seemed necessary.

The revolutionaries said the Tsar was safe, he did not count, he was stupid, and his survival helped their cause more than could his death. They meant this in a sinister way. They meant: the Tsar by his wickedness and folly shows more clearly than we could show by propaganda that the day of Tsars is over and that it is better for mankind to dispense with Tsars altogether. The revolutionaries were wholly mistaken.

The Tsar's life and personal character are a mystery. He is beyond definite comment in his own country. Unless he shows himself, no one can say what he is. It

L   161

remains till now to make a fair estimate of his ideals and his passion. The Tsar to-day has outlived the accusation of insincerity, has outlived all his unpopularity, and has given the lie to all that has been said against him. He has no doubt gone through great spiritual evolution in these parlous and suffering times. His mind has been working all the time, and to-day he emerges as a great serious monarch whose entire thought and continuous anxiety have been "What must be done to save my people from their dangers, and to put them on the high road of a great destiny?"

The personal work of the Tsar shows itself in the courageous attack which he made on the great corrupt police system which had sold itself in part to the revolutionary party. The police system in Russia is in some respects more powerful than the Tsardom itself, and it can almost always procure the assassination of its persecutors. The Tsar very seriously endangered his life by his efforts. Next was the more peaceful but less easy problem of giving more land to the peasants and settling them on small holdings. Next was the extraordinary manifesto against drunkenness made in the spring of this year, when the Imperial sanction was given to a campaign for local veto and several hundred thousand vodka shops were closed. In passing, let us remember the amnesty given to revolutionary exiles, permitting Gorky, among others, to return to Russia unharmed. Then there was the Tsar and the war, the noble proclamations and brother's hand extended towards Poland, the religious pilgrimage to the famous Russian shrines to pray for Russia, and the complete abolition by Imperial ukase of the sale of vodka, first for a month, then for the space of the duration of the war, and now—by promise—for ever.

Sacred Simplicity

So on the day when Turkey stepped into the arena of war, the great street-mobs of Moscow and Petrograd carry the Tsar's portrait through the capitals, singing "God save the Tsar" and cheering and shouting with indescribable enthusiasm. To-day, the Tsar goes about his kingdom unguarded and without precautions. He goes without hesitation to the front, to the inspiriting of his soldiers at Ossovetz. He visits Roman Catholic and Polish Vilna and salutes there the emblems of Catholicism and Polish nationalism.

When some years ago I wrote in the middle of "Undiscovered Russia"—"God save the Tsar!" it was taken as a paradox and even quoted against the book by one formidable Radical journal. To-day, "God save the Tsar!" is a clamorous sentiment of the Russian streets.

Before the Tsar passed the uniform for the common soldier in the war he asked that a complete suit be sent to him, and with it boots and rifle and full kit. And he himself took off his royal clothes and put on the soldier's uniform and shouldered the kit and the gun and walked in them on his estate in Livadia some two hours. He was photographed so, and has allowed the photograph to be reproduced for common sale and for distribution among the soldiers.

He is a simple man. He inherits the awful power of his ancestors, but he would like to spend a day as a common soldier in the trenches. Such an action would resound throughout history and win the hearts of the whole non-German world. But necessarily, the Tsar is to the peasants someone unearthly, a giant, a demigod. They would not really be well influenced by such an action, probably would not understand it. Still, who knows? Noble deeds take care of themselves.

Russia and the World

As the war goes on, the sincerity and the nobility of the Tsar will be a great factor in the giving of victory. The sacred simplicity, kindness, and earnestness of the Tsar emerge as a guarantee of the ultimate issue of this struggle, but also of the marvellous and healthful future of the vast Russian Empire and of the wonderful Russian people. It is good to see in the idealist, the Peace Tsar, the same personality of to-day, but made wiser, stronger, simpler by suffering and responsibility—the Great White Tsar.

M. SAZONOF

THOUGH I have never been in the capital before, I have friends there, thanks to my books, which stand for me to those who have not met me. It is very pleasant to meet people who have an intimate knowledge of you even before they have seen your face. At Petrograd I had such a pleasant meeting with Madame Sazonof and her husband, the Foreign Minister, with one of the ladies-in-waiting on the Empress, and with Madame Novikof, so full of years and yet so energetic, M.P. for Russia, as Disraeli called her. Madame Novikof I had met in London; the others I met for the first time.

I was very glad to see the Russian Minister for Foreign Affairs face to face, and to come into personal contact with a man whose voice counts for so much in the councils of Russia and of the Allies. A hard man, yet kindly, brisk, alert, European. You would not say you were in the presence of a Russian except for the conversational vivacity of the Minister, and a certain Slavonic impulsiveness which lurks only half suppressed, half masked in the eyes of this strong and determined man. He has an English manner, an English way of living, and evidently has a strong personal liking for English things and English ways. He has lived eight years in England in his time, and so knows us pretty well. He, as much as anyone on either side, realises the value of mutual friendship, not only now when we can co-operate with soldiers and cannon and sailors and ships, but afterwards, for the working out together of the problems of peace.

I had a pleasant hour's talk at the Minister's house in the Downing Street of Petrograd, a fine old crimson walled mansion on the Dvortsovy Proyezd.

You enter from a door parallel to that which leads to the department. A lackey meets you; you are put into a tiny lift and slowly raised to a parquet-floored gallery leading to a bright reception room warmed and illumined by an open log fire. Madame Sazonof came forward to meet me, and with her an interesting pet dog, a Siberian *laika*, that walked behind me and caught my instep in his mouth each time I lifted my right foot.

"He is finding out about you," said Madame Sazonof with a smile. "He always makes sure of every one who comes here. He almost frightened the Austrian Ambassador away altogether, and in the days before the war the Ambassador used to send up to have the dog taken away before he would make his appearance."

"He knew who was the enemy," said I.

"Yes, you see, now, he quite takes to you."

I barked at him. We were soon on very friendly terms and he sat on his tail all through luncheon and looked up into my eyes, and I was advised to give him some titbits, which I did.

M. Sazonof came in and we spoke together in Russian. But when we went in to luncheon, an English luncheon by the way, we all spoke English. The Russians spoke so well and so charmingly that you might imagine you were listening to a party of English talking in a similar circle in London.

The Minister made light of the danger of being

The Tsar alone with his People

attacked in London by our Russophobes. What he feared in going to England was the Channel crossing, no more. He thought I might have a bad time going home, might get captured by the Germans, and he thought I had better stay in Russia. I said I thought of going by Archangel, but he assured me it was closed by ice.

We talked of the Tsar. "I wonder if people in England realise what a great thing the vodka prohibition is?" said Sazonof. "We are sober from end to end. We look for extraordinary results when once the war is over and we have time to develop in peace."

"It is making the Tsar very popular," said I. "Even in our country many of those who have felt themselves out of sympathy with Russia begin to point to the Tsar as to an ideal monarch."

"Isn't the Tsar splendid?" said a young Baroness who was present; and she told a story of the Tsar visiting a hospital in Poland, and talking with the soldiers.

"He entered the hospital accompanied by many officials and court dignitaries, and passed with them in one of the great general rooms, where lay several hundred wounded men. The chief surgeon was about to show him round, when the Tsar, evidently in great emotion, turned to him and the rest of the decorated officials around him and said: 'Leave me here alone.' They bowed and scraped, but did not, however, go out. 'Leave me here alone with the soldiers,' said the Tsar again; 'I wish to speak to them myself.' When he had said these words the surgeon and the rest slowly, and as it were unwillingly, went out, and the Tsar was left alone with his poor wounded soldiers; and he talked with them for a whole hour. So he got rid of that terrible old background of official Russia, and was himself. Don't you think it a beautiful picture of the Tsar alone with his people?"

"The Tsar has a beautiful character," said Madame Sazonof. "Every one who comes into touch with him personally, feels his tenderness toward his fellow men, his delicate consideration for all people with whom he has to deal."

After lunch we adjourned to a beautiful old room, warmed and lit by a log fire burning on a large hearth. Here we had coffee, and I chatted with the Minister by the fire; whilst the ladies sat round a table beside one of the great windows and talked. Among other things that Sazonof said were the following:

"I hope you are making up your minds to have a larger army, not only now, but after the war is over. Your fleet is splendid. It is surpassing all expectations, but your army was far too weak when the war broke out, and is too weak for your Imperial needs.

"I think that, as the years go on, there will be even greater scope for Russian and British friendship than before. We have yet to know one another better, of course. There is really no room for jealousy between the two Empires.

"What is the feeling in your country about the settlement? How do they look now at Constantinople? We should much prize the opinion, not only of the British Government, but of the British people; for we realise that, when peace is made, it will be a peace between peoples as much, and even more, than between Governments."

I asked about the autonomy of Poland, and the position of the Jews there. I suggested that something be done to help out the Jews who wish to go to America.

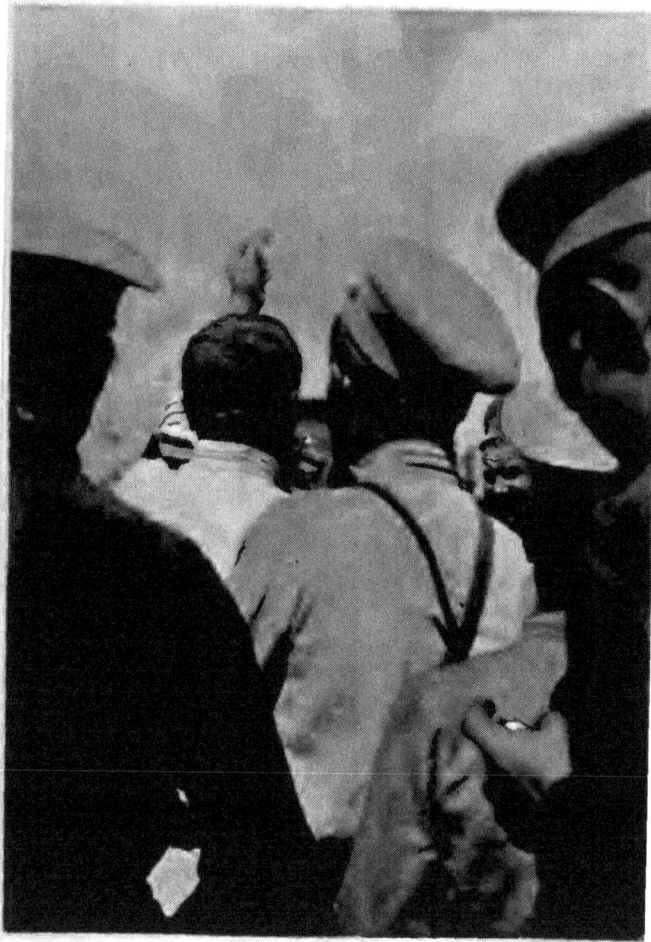

Dancing round the Rouble: Cossack shows the
Tsar's head on the silver coin, while the
others sing the National Anthem and dance
round.

Scope for British Friendship

"They are not likely to go in great numbers," said he. "They don't want to go. They had much rather settle in Russia or in Siberia."

"Is anything likely to be done to relieve the tension of the Jewish problem?"

M. Sazonof thought it possible that they might be excused military service in future if they wished it. He recognised the great difficulty of dealing with the Jewish problem, but spoke enthusiastically of the coming restoration of Poland. Russia ought to have made up the quarrel with the suffering Poles long ago.

Finally, we spoke of the prospect of Russo-British friendship, and of the mutual co-operation of the two great Powers in Asia. He thought that with the war the old Asiatic rivalry would completely disappear. Russian civilisation was a help to British civilisation. The Christian churches on the North of the Himalayas were brother churches of the English on the other side.

A rather amusing thing happened to me the day after I had seen Sazonof. A secret agent took me apart and said:

"You saw Sazonof yesterday; what did you think of him—is he a strong man?"

"Yes, a strong man I should say, with plenty of common sense. Of course, he knows where to look to take his cue."

The agent lowered his voice and said in a hushed whisper:

"Where would you say he looked, to Baron——?" and he mentioned a certain influential German Russian supposed to be carrying on an intrigue in favour of peace.

"Why, no," said I, "to the Tsar I meant, of course."

And I felt like a person speaking in some novel of diplomatic life.

THE GRAND DUKE NIKOLAÏ

VERY briefly I should like to refer to the Grand Duke Nikolaï, whose father was a brother of Alexander III. In the Russian army the Grand Duke has the rank of a demi-god rather than of a man. He is above all intrigue, and his word in the war is as powerful as that of the Tsar. He is a man of great personal character—quick, determined, capable. He is 6 ft. 3 in. in height, and has a fine presence. He has the reputation of being very severe, and will stand no nonsense. Many officers who have failed in their duty he has degraded to the ranks.

He is a great success, and is very highly thought of by Kitchener and French and Joffre. He is also the surprise of the war. Nobody had heard anything of him before. As Madame Novikof writes to me from Petrograd: "The present hero of the day has taken the world by surprise. Nobody knew him in his real greatness."

.

THE VODKA PROHIBITION

THE Russian nation spent £9,000,000 more on vodka in the year 1913-14 than in 1912-13. It spent £50,000,000 more than it did ten years ago. The population increased by some thirty per cent. in ten years, but the sale of vodka fifty per cent. According to the estimate of Count Witte, made in February, 1914, in the Gosudarstvenny Sovet, or Council of State, the nation would have spent during the current financial year no less than £100,000,000 on strong drink.

These figures, growing steadily more alarming year by year, at last necessitated a broad national consideration of the whole subject of temperance. For some months in 1914 Russia talked of nothing but the struggle against drunkenness.

Count Witte, who was responsible for the acquirement by the Russian Government of the monopoly—i.e. of the whole business of selling vodka, an excellent measure, both financially and morally—came forward to defend his good name and to point out to the Government that the time was ripe for their turning the liquor control to the moral benefit of the nation. A great many people are ready to ascribe to Count Witte the blame of the increasing Russian insobriety—even Socialists, to whom one would think the idea of State control would be especially pleasing, are ready to cast that aspersion. But, obviously, Russia had everything to gain by this simplification of the whole vast trade of selling spirits. At the Tsar's word, in this place or in that, in this province or that district, the sale of vodka could be forbidden.

"If I had now the power of approach to His Majesty as a member of the Government," said Count Witte, "I would advise His Majesty, without waiting for the decision of the Duma or of the Council of State, to publish a ukase to the effect that His Majesty now finds it indispensable to lay the foundation of Russian temperance by limiting the gross sale of vodka to £900,000,000."

The balance of superfluous revenue, strange to say, Count Witte would have given to temperance societies—£10,000,000 to Bands of Hope. No Government outside a novel would part with such an immense sum of money to amateur societies, though, of course, the Young Men's Christian Association would do a great deal for sobriety with £10,000,000.

A great number of people went much further than Count Witte, and said : "Forbid the sale altogether, forbid it in certain districts, forbid it in certain provinces for a start, or allow local option." But the late Premier, M. Kokovtsoff, generally negatived these proposals by his fear of the outbreak of general illicit trading in spirits, and his disinclination to deprive those who already drink temperately. He did not look for, nor indeed expect, the complete abstinence of the Russian nation—did anyone?

Russia, however, was in a position of real difficulty. Her industrial villages, and those barracks of workmen and workwomen that have sprung up around great country factories were in such a state on Sundays and festivals that it was extremely unpleasant, and sometimes dangerous, for a well-dressed person to pass through them. They were infested with mobs of hooligans; up and down the main street a dozen men and as many women might be found yelling, singing, screeching like demented creatures. In almost every house someone would be drunk; yet in the remoter agricultural villages you would seldom come across anything of the kind. It was the accompaniment of better wages, lack of pleasure in factory life, lack of the education which a peasant can do without but which a factory worker must have. But it was something more than mere weakness, it was a menace to respectable society. No paper could ever dream of recording a tenth of the assaults, murders, robberies, and obscenities that occurred in the industrial cities and villages and factory-barracks of Russia. They were unchronicled.

Before the Tsar stepped in the Russian Government had only an old remedy—to imprison offenders. Many people thought that though imprisonment was a wrong method it was indeed efficacious. But the astonishing truth was dawning on the Russian people that if Russia had ten times as many prisons it could not accommodate its wrongdoers. The police all over the country knew that it was no use arresting drunkards and assaulters. If they arrested them there was no place to put them; they could only be reprimanded and released. In Vladikavkaz not so long ago there was a drunken fray in the main street, stabbing, firing of revolvers; some twenty or thirty people · were arrested, but there was nothing to be done with them; they were all released.

"Siberia is vast," said some. But already Siberia claims to be a young living State, and notifies Russia that she must no longer be treated as a penal settlement.

A great deal of money has been voted each year for the encouragement of sobriety; and in the spring one of the Moscow papers made a special inquiry in every province of what was being done with the money, and printed a most interesting report.

At Nizhni Novgorod Fair the authorities had established a temperance museum, two reading-rooms, two tea-houses, an open-air theatre, and a home for drunkards. Almost every province had established a whole series of village reading-rooms, generally in the post office, and spread on long tables many anti-alcohol sheets and church papers. The literature was deeply uninteresting, and I may say that I have visited many such free libraries and have rarely found anyone reading there. In many places, however, cinematograph shows were arranged, and to them the population flocked; amateur theatricals were planned, farces and operettas were performed, the tango was danced, and the latest comic song was brought down. In some rare cases evening classes were arranged. In the Jewish Pale free legal help was given.

All but one of the reports sent in indicated that, despite large amounts of money voted for temperance aid, drunkenness was strongly on the increase; and for that reason there was some doubt as to the advisability of giving another 10,000,000 roubles to the cause.

There were real natural forces fighting against drunkenness, and winning—the lighting up of personal ambition, the cinematograph, the Evangelical movement. The Church of Russia, though it did not exclude the drunkard or evil-doer, stood steadily for sobriety. It did not say it was a sin to drink, and, indeed, its own priests drank lustily—even to excess upon occasion—but it stood utterly against brutal drunkenness. It may seem strange to English people to differentiate; but there is a difference between the drunkenness which comes from melancholy or from true sociability and the drunkenness which is just beastliness, the drunkenness with which are associated coarseness, lying, fighting, and stealing—the difference between being "drunk as a lord" and "drunk as a Kaffir." It is against the latter that Russia has to fight. It can never, without racial change, get rid of its melancholy and its social spirit.

Kharkov, they say, abounds in temperance brother-hoods. Theosophy is on the increase, also vegetarianism, and evangelism. All these make for sobriety. It is somewhat saddening to see the rents in the Church since religious freedom was granted in Russia. But there is true consolation in the fact that the flocking converts are earnest men and women who feel they want to lead a new life. They take our Western forms and ethics; they despise the drunkard, they are puritanical in judgment, but they are a hardening and strengthening power in the nation.

A most extraordinary phenomenon, the Russian nation's sudden passion for sobriety! It seemed something passing, something merely of the moment when it first gave notice of itself in Press articles and public speeches. But when the Tsar gave his famous rescript to M. Bark asking him to limit the sale of vodka, and when what was practically a national measure of local veto was adopted, the whole of Russia from Tsar to peasant woman was swept with a temperance ardour.

Long before the war thousands of spirit shops had been sealed owing to popular demand. The drunkards themselves petitioned to have the vodka supply cut off. For those with an eye to the future of Russia this was an astonishingly significant spectacle.

Still Russia was a long way off from national sobriety. We looked for something else to combat desire for drink. Russia would have to survey her industrial regions and drain her human marshes systematically. The gold - mining villages, for instance, still remained what they were. It seemed evident that something more drastic would have to be done.

The drastic thing arrived. The war broke out and at once, by Imperial ukase, every vodka shop in the kingdom was closed, the sale of vodka in restaurants and in railway buffets was prohibited, and at a stroke of the pen vodka was unobtainable. Contrary to expectation, there was not even any illicit trading in spirits—at least none to speak of. Russia was made sober not by act of Parliament, but by something more powerful than that, more ready, more simple—by word of Tsar.

In the early days of the hostilities it was a commonplace to thank God for the German declaration of war; it had closed as if by magic every spirit shop in Russia and Siberia. It had liberated town and countryside from the dreariness of drink.

Great days for the *Tresveniki*, a Russian sect that preaches nothing but temperance. It was founded by a simple Moscow man who gathered an enormous number of adherents, orthodox as well as Russian nonconformists. They drew up the great petition, which, after ten weeks of the war and of enforced sobriety, was presented to the Tsar, a petition for the prohibition of vodka for ever.

It seemed preposterous to ask the Tsar for complete prohibition in the face of Russia's tremendous war debts. The Tsar had promised that no more vodka should be sold until the end of the war; and that promise had been greeted with great satisfaction. It had been taken as a maximum. The hope was that, even after the war, vodka would never be sold in the old easy way, at a moderate price in small bottles, to whoever asked for it.

But the impossible happened. The Tsar not only received the petitioners, but answered them in the following significant sentence :

"I had already decided on total prohibition before I read your petition."

So Russia was rejoiced by the Tsar, by one of the most amazing personal acts in the modern history of civilisation.

And it is a fact the vodka shop is closed. Many people in England seem inclined to doubt the reality of this measure ; but I can vouch for it, who have seen Russia sober. Not only has the sale of vodka been stopped, but the sale of beer also. It is impossible to find a drunken man on a festival, or on an ordinary day, anywhere in the Russian Empire, except in the Caucasus and parts of Central Asia, where the Government has never held the monopoly of the sale of intoxicating liquors. It is quiet in the industrial villages, in the "factories," and in the mining settlements. The old songs are sung; there is the old sociability, but it is over tea and around the samovar. In every province of Russia there has been an astonishing decrease in crime, in the breaking of heads, in immorality. The papers in the great cities continually have to spare columns in their war-filled issues, in order to give the facts of sobriety, and comment on them. Russia is greatly pleased with herself as a non-drinking nation.

The great question is: Will complete prohibition be feasible after the war is over? Will not the warriors returning from victory demand drinks to toast the Tsar and the Allies and their generals? Will there be vodka riots, or will the men who return be ready to sacrifice their old habits for the national ideal? I am inclined to think that it will be the latter. The soldiers will almost unanimously approve thé prohibition. I talked to several soldiers about it. One, who was attached to the aviation service, as the servant of an officer, gives me an example of what the peasants are thinking. He had bought a loaf and two herrings, and, eating them with great gusto, exclaimed: " Ah, for some vodka now."

" You'd like some, eh?"

"Lots of us are like madmen because we can't get it."

"Tell me, what do you think of shutting up the spirit shop? Would you like to have it open again?"

"No, I wouldn't."

" Why?"

"Why! Because the spirit shop is our enemy. If you have a quarter in your pocket and the door of the shop is open, in you go. You don't want to go, but if the door's open you can't help yourself. If you know the door's open in a village five miles away—you go there and buy the vodka. And what's the good of it after all? No, brother, we've learned something in this war. I, for instance, have been flying in the air. None of our village has ever flown. Who would have dreamed of me going up among the clouds and the stars like a Frenchman or an Englishman? There you see what noble Allies we have. They don't drink, why should we?"

" Didn't you feel frightened going up so high?"

" Yes, first time it was rather dreadful, but that was only for a few minutes. It's nothing to go up now."

" Did you fly over the enemy?"

" Yes, one day at Novo-Georgievsk we set out to

learn which way the Germans were moving towards Warsaw, and we flew over them. Lord! how little those Germans looked, but they all began to fire at us, with rifles and field guns and cannon, and, as one or two bullets went through our sails, we went higher, and turned away and came back home."

"Didn't you feel afraid?"

"Not a little bit."

"What are you going to do now?"

"I am being sent to escort a new aeroplane to the front."

"And you can get on without vodka?"

"Yes, long as I have my wife with me."

"What do you mean—your wife?"

"Yes, my wife goes everywhere with me now. When I lie down at night she is there beside me, and when I waken up in the morning there she is still." He pointed to his rifle and smiled.

I might give many talks, and as far as they touched on the vodka question there was always the same sentiment—though the soldiers would give anything for a drink, yet they are glad that it was impossible to get it.

Still, it is certain that, if the peasant is deprived of his vodka, and that means of drowning his sorrows and escaping from his ennui, something must be done to make up for the loss. Especially in the industrial villages, holidays without vodka will be dreary beyond words. The industrial communities must be given a share in the advantages of industrialism. The people must be given personal ambition, art, literature, music. Instead of the tango, the performance of indecent farces and tinkling operettas, the foreign and thought-confusing cinema, must come fundamental education, good libraries,

Russia and the World

good theatres, music. From my knowledge of the Russian peasantry, I know nothing that would so effectively combat drunkenness and hooliganism as the establishment of musical societies and bands in every village in the country. The Russians are surely the most musical people in the world. At village cinema theatres, where before or after the shadow-show there has been a trio or quartet with guitars or balalaikas, I have seen drunken peasants stand up in the front row and try to make long declamations to the musicians, whilst all through the pictures they have sat staring into vacancy and wondering dimly where they were. Music awakens the best soul of the Russian. When he is dead drunk he will raise his ear to a song.

If Russia is going to be truly strong in this matter she has got to raise a new generation who not only deny vodka, but who would not enter the vodka shop even if the door were open. But, whatever happens, temperate Russia will have a great deal more driving power, will be more ambitious, and more able to get what it wants in the world than dear, melancholy drunken Russia.

DISTRUST OF RUSSIA OR FRIENDSHIP WITH RUSSIA

IT is very strange, but many of those who in public life stand first of all for peace and goodwill have yet an unappeasable malice against Russia. When war broke out a number of the Pacifists, Mr. Llewellyn Williams among them, came forward honourably and said: We did not see that Germany was the enemy, did not see that at the last we should be bound to fight her, and we were wrong. England is proud of men who have the courage to come out like Mr. Williams; such men are the strength of England. But what of the remainder of the Pacifist party—it was thought to be dead? It became stone-silent for awhile. Russia was fêted: Germany was cried against. We went forward in our might to shield Belgium and France from the common enemy. We seemed to fail somewhat; Paris was in danger. On the other hand, the Russians began to go ahead in East Prussia; they took town after town and even threatened Berlin. Germany was obliged to give the Russian invasion her serious attention. It was the general opinion that the Russian onslaught saved Paris and made possible for French and English the great victory of the Marne. No one in England dare attack Russia, even in a veiled way.

Then Germany, realising that the three Powers, England, France and Russia, were too strong for her, sought by cunning to separate them. A rumour was set abroad that Russia was about to make a secret peace, that the Tsar when he went to Ossovets really went to try to arrange a pact with the Germans. During the black days of Warsaw it was whispered that Russia had sold Warsaw to the Germans. When the Germans were driven back to Mlava and Neidenburg and Thorn it was rumoured that Germany had agreed to evacuate Poland and then discuss terms of secret peace. During all the sanguinary struggle in Poland that ensued it has been hinted that Russia was only playing at fighting. Fortunately, the English Censor recognised that this was German propaganda designed to bring about distrust between England and Russia. Nine-tenths of the journalists in Russia, not knowing the Russian language or having any intimate realisation of Russian character, swallowed the interesting stories and wrote them to London and to New York. They put them in their journalistic correspondence, they put them in their letters. Some, of course, got through. And they brought to speech and to life the Russophobe and Pacifist party whom every one thought to be dead.

It was said that Russia did not intend to redeem her promise to Poland, that she was getting swelled head through her victories, that she was capable of selling the liberties of Europe. Most insidiously of all, it was hinted that, when we had humbled Germany, we should have to turn our attention to Russia. It was Russia's turn next to be isolated and humbled.

A reasonable person necessarily asked: Might it not possibly turn out to be England's turn to be isolated and humbled? When has England shown herself so capable a diplomatist, or Russia so poor a diplomatist, that it should be possible to isolate Russia?

Shaw and Russia

Bernard Shaw, who for fifteen years has had more than anyone else the ear of the British public, and has been trying to educate the British public, and give to it his own point of view, did a great deal to ferment distrust of Russia by a pamphlet which the Censor might justifiably have emended. Had a journal in Russia dared to print similar animadversions upon England and the Allies, it would have been confiscated and the editor brought into court and fined. According to Mr. Shaw:—

"Russia has been able to set all three Western friends and neighbours, Germany, France, and England, shedding rivers of blood from one another's throats.

"The Russian Government is the open enemy of every liberty we boast of.

"Under Russian government, people whose worst crime is to find the *Daily News* a congenial newspaper are hanged, flogged, or sent to Siberia as a matter of daily routine." This, Mr. Shaw, who pride yourself on being normal, is an absurd lie, a hateful lie, seeing that it is intended for the ears of those who are wont not to think for themselves. The *Russkia Vedimosti* and the *Retch* are journals of a much more irreconcilable type than the *Daily News;* but who has ever been flogged or hanged or even fined for reading them?

"Russia has been welcome to flog and hang her H. G. Wellses and Lloyd Georges by the dozen without a word of remonstrance from our plutocratic Press." Not one of Mr. H. G. Wells's books, all of which are translated, has been stopped in Russia.

"My heart," says G. B. S., "is with the Moscow Art Theatre." I had thought it was rather with some Vienna or Berlin theatre, where his works are usually produced before they are produced in England. As to

Russia and the World

the Art Theatre at Moscow, it produced one play of Shaw's long ago as an experiment—*Cæsar and Cleopatra*. But for the last ten years he has not written a play that had any interest to the Moscow Theatre of Art.

"My heart is with the Russia of Tolstoy, and Turgenieff, and Dostoieffsky, and Gorky, and Tchekof." How Mr. Shaw's intellect has been at variance with his heart, then. His heart is with Dostoieffsky. Dostoieffsky's heart was a large one—it sheltered Raskolnikof and Ivan Karamazof and even Smerdyakof. It sheltered, however, no Germans.

"When we fight the Tsar we are fighting not for Tolstoy and Gorky, but for the forces that Tolstoy thundered against all his life"—And when the Tsar is fighting for us, Mr. Shaw!

"I know all our disinterested and thoughtful supporters of the war feel deeply uneasy about the Russian alliance." The wish is father to the thought.

"Until Russia becomes a federation of several separate democratic states, and the Tsar is either promoted to the honourable position of hereditary President or else totally abolished, the Eastern boundary of the League of Peace must be the Eastern boundary of Swedish, German and Italian civilisation." In other words, a league of peace, i.e. an alliance, must be formed between England and Germany and the rest after the war, but Russia must be dropped, Russia must be isolated, and, if necessary, fought by the League of Peace.

"A victory unattainable without Russian aid would be a defeat for Western European Liberalism." To this I say—let Liberals speak for themselves. Mr. Shaw is a Socialist—the very opposite of a Liberal. For the rest, I would ask those who agree with Mr. Shaw, which would be the greater defeat, this so-called moral defeat, or the actual defeat which would have taken place if the three Emperors had been in alliance—Germany, Russia, and Austria, against England and France?

"Our allies of to-day may be our enemies of to-morrow."

Many Russians reading these opinions will think that Mr. Shaw may have been bought by the Germans to write them. They are wrong. These are Shaw's actual thoughts, inspired by his vanity and his hate of religion. On the other hand, many Russians will think that Shaw's opinion is representative of British opinion, and they will conclude that we are not true friends of Russia, that we are ready to betray her the moment our own security is achieved. The pamphlet should have been stopped. Its immediate effect is to strengthen the hand of the German party at the Russian court and to put us in danger of having to fight, not only Germany and Austria, which are already as much as we can manage, but Russia as well. Such a pamphlet as Mr. Shaw's is a blow to Russian freedom, Russian hope, in fact to the very forces in Russia with whom Mr. Shaw alleges his heart is to be found.

Everything is to be gained by being generous to Russia, by knowing her and loving her, and consequently trusting her utterly. What men like Shaw and the haters of Russia try to spread is ignorance of Russia. True knowledge of Russia means love towards her, tenderness, generosity. The truly religious heart of England looks to find strength, spiritual food, inspiration, and when it comes to Russia it finds it. Socialists of the Shaw type have a great malice against religion. All materialists and humanitarians see in Russia the enemy. Hence the lies

Russia and the World

about her flogging her H. G. Wellses. Hence the insistence on the persecution of the Jews. Some of these pacifist people, so full of peace and goodwill when the cost of armaments is under discussion, yet fan every little flame of hate against Russia, and one might imagine that if the little flame led to a conflagration of war between us and Russia they would be in the front rank of rejoicers. Not they! They would slink off and let the ignorant masses whom they had gulled shout the cheers for war.

Thanks to the English friends of Russia and the Russian friends of England we are fighting on one side to-day for a common end. And Russia is our staunch friend. She enables us to defeat the Germans. Those who are whispering treason against Russia are those who in time of peace did everything to weaken us. They were poisoning our youth and spoiling our women with indecent novels and plays; they were turning our national attention exclusively upon the mentally deficient, the aged, the slum-dwellers; they were doing their best to stop the growth of the Navy and to undermine the loyalty of the Army. They were discouraging Imperial unity and Colonial friendship. They have done their best to damage Anglo-Russian friendship, collecting the riff-raff of German Jews and Russian subjects fled from Russian justice, some of them political idealists and honourable peace-loving citizens, but many drawn from the criminal class of the East End,* to protest in the name of England against Russian domestic and Imperial policy.

* A great deal of East End crime, such as the Tottenham outrages, the Houndsditch murders, the Stinie Morrison (alias Stein) affair, have been associated with Russian subjects—not with pure Russians, it is true, but with members of Russia's subject races.

Love Russia

There is room for liberal thought about Russia. True Liberals are most precious to us. We need to be reminded of the rights of small nations to fulfil their national destinies, and not be absorbed into large empires. Behold, Liberals have the ear of Russia! It is a Liberal Government that represents England in the Anglo-Russian friendship. Liberals have inestimable power to help Russia—by loving her, not by criticising and attacking her. I would say to Liberals: Read Dostoieffsky, and Tchekof, and Kouprin, and Gorky and Sologub, read my own story of the Russian pilgrims; go to Russia, talk to Russians, but do not read Shaw on Russia, or other pessimists on Russia, and do not go to Jews and talk to them of Russia. By the negative side, even if it be a true negative side, you cannot know Russia. There is something stronger than *nagaikas* and pogroms that keeps the Tsardom together —the Tsardom that survived the terrible Japanese War and was still strong enough to overcome the greatest revolutionary movement of modern times. Knowing Russia, you will find a common ground. Knowing and loving Russia, spiritual forces will flow into your life and your destiny. Russia known and loved by you will profit by your long Western experience, your trained hand and practical intelligence. All Liberals who are true Liberals, and wish from their hearts the welfare of small nations and of individuals, and who would always safeguard to these the opportunity to fulfil their national and individual destiny, should take these words to heart. In the case of nations and individuals affected by the government of Russia you can help them most by loving and trusting Russia. You do not help them at all; on the contrary, you frustrate them by remaining ignorant of mighty Russia, attacking her, threatening her.

Russia and the World

As it is among individual friends, so it is among national friends. If you love Russia, she will love you in return; if you trust her, she will trust you; if you are generous to her, she will never be outdone in generosity.

> The song is to the singer, and comes back most to him,
> The gift is to the giver, and comes back most to him,
> The love is to the lover, and comes back most to him,
>   —it cannot fail.

THE SETTLEMENT OF PEACE

WE are at war with Germany, and, for the time being, with the German Idea. We are at war with German ruthlessness, with that barbarism that does not stay the German as he rushes rough-shod over other nations' holy ground. We are at war with Germany's disregard for other people's feelings, with Germany's wish to Germanise territory and nations that have no sympathy with Germany or German culture. Consequently, when the war closes with victory over Germany we must hope that it will close with victory over the German Idea also. Peace, when we make it, should be peace over the ruins of Germany; it should also be peace over the beaten and frustrated German Idea. Let us be on our guard lest, though we beat Germany, the German Idea gain the better over us, win our sympathy and. enter into alliance with our thoughts. We fight like Englishmen, let us make peace like Englishmen.

At least, let us not make for ourselves the sort of peace that Germans would have made for themselves had they won.

Our true peace as Englishmen, Frenchmen and Russians should be a peace founded on a love of differences and a reverence for distinguishing marks. In difference we see a divine manifestation of the God who makes both the daisy and the rose, and the tiger and the mouse, and the eagle and the mole, each perfection of its kind. Difference is God's beauty and the sign of His creative fingers. It is difference that thrills us towards life—similarity and monotony that cause us to become dull and to die. Tacitus wrote of a conqueror that he made a desert and called it peace—that was a German peace. We will not make a silence and call it peace, or a great collective State, or an Empire over enslaved nations, but instead, we will make a singing, and give land and freedom to small nations and let them live under their own little flags and speak their own language and chant the poems of their own song-books. Poles shall be Poles and shall not call themselves Russians, Jews shall call themselves Jews, and not Russians or Germans or English. They can call themselves Americans, but then America is a nation in synthesis. America is the melting-pot where pure types are lost in order that a new type may be brought forth. Finns shall be Finns, and shall realise themselves in Finland. The Slavs shall escape from the Austrian yoke, but shall not thereby fall under the yoke of the Great Russians. The Belgians shall be set on their feet once more. Alsace shall be free to be French. Power to change nationality shall be withheld. No Germans, Russians, Jews, Poles, and so forth shall be allowed to masquerade as British under legal recognisance of a change of nationality. Ireland and Ulster shall both be free.

International understanding is often very like matrimonial understanding. It occurs that those people who rush to marriage with the joy of feeling themselves alike in every way, find afterwards that there are many dissimilarities, and one tries to enslave the other's personality, or there is an open rupture. The understanding that is best founded and is likely to last longest is that which is founded on a love of the differences in the two personalities.

There is a remarkable assumption in modern writers, especially in Socialist writers, that all nations are in themselves much of a muchness, alike in ideals, in temperament, and in possibility. According to these it is only the waywardness of certain Governments, like the British Government or the Russian Government, that stands in the path towards uniformity. They see ahead one language, one State for the whole of the world. That is the Socialist ideal. Those who have read "The World Set Free" may remember how every character in the story, however foreign his name, is still in temperament an Englishman. Little stock is taken of the wonderful differences which separate as yet all the nations of Europe; the differences in instinct, the necessary differences in destiny and in expression. The Socialist World-State is formed, and there is seemingly no rebellion against its uniformities. All use of weapons and of war is reserved to the police, who will suppress at once any rebellion against the service of the World-State. To quote Bernard Shaw, who is one of the leaders of the Socialists in England:—

"You will reserve your shrapnel for the wasters who shirk their share of the industrial service of their country"; or again,

"I hold no brief for small States as such. We are in no way bound to knight-errantry on their behalf against big ones."

Liberals live on friendly terms with Socialists. But in this great hour of testing they will probably try many opinions of their Socialist acquaintances and find them in opposition to true Liberalism—true Liberalism being respect for the differences in individuals and in nations; respect for the rights of individuals to follow out as they wish their God-given destiny; respect for the rights of small nations to follow out as they will their destiny also.

In this war, that is during the fighting of it, Conservatives and Liberals alike in Russia and in Great Britain have found a common ground. That common ground will avail them as advantageously in the settlement of peace after the war is over.

If each individual will work out his political creed and see where he stands, and how he personally would like to settle the war, I feel sure that a great number will come to the following conclusion: what we want at the end of the war is not a bargain peace, not a wretched patched up affair, but a lasting and just peace founded on a great principle. We need to establish the principle of nationality before we work out the details. One of the chief reasons for promoting the mutual love and understanding between Russia and France and Britain is that the Allies may meet in that spirit of friendship that will enable them to establish that principle. If they meet in distrust or selfishness after the war, then it will be only a wretched bargain peace that will be arranged, a series of diplomatic victories or defeats for one nation or another.

The details of peace will in any case be difficult to work out. The redistribution of Europe is a great and difficult task. It will need much delicate intelligence to demarcate the new boundary lines, to know how "to take occasion by the hand," to know what functions may be given to each young State, to safeguard against immediate jealousy and resumption of war on a petty scale. When the war is over it will probably be better for each and all of us that it be really over for a while. We British at least will try to give the world a clean slate and start the nations without any debts or grudges—all trespasses forgiven.

The most honourable terms of peace would be perhaps the following :—

Germany give to Belgium Aix-la-Chapelle and Cologne, and also sufficient of a war indemnity to start her on her feet again.

Britain ask no return of the money she has given to Belgium, Russia and France, or of the money she has herself spent on the fighting.

Part of German Poland—not all, for that would mean coming within fifty miles of Berlin—be added to the whole of Austrian and Russian Poland, and a Russian protectorate or Polish independent kingdom be established.

Russia's right of entry into the Mediterranean be established ; Constantinople be put under Russian protection, and the Cathedral of St. Sophia given to the Russian Orthodox Church ; St. Sophia so becoming the St. Peter's of the Eastern Orthodox Church—one arm being the Patriarchates of Jerusalem and Constantinople, the other the Patriarchate of Moscow.

Alsace-Lorraine be given back to the French.

The Jews be put at liberty to form a Jewish Government in Palestine, and Jews all the world over be given the option of becoming Jewish subjects.

The German Fleet be taken over by her present foes and divided between them in lieu of war indemnity—so lessening the terrible financial burdens which threaten to stifle German science and culture after the war. We need Germany shining in the new Europe. Germany extinguished would be a real loss.

Japan have a protectorate over Tsing-Tau and be guaranteed from European molestation in China and the Pacific.

German African colonies be restored to Germany.

Most of these terms can be obtained if the Allies co-operate in a friendly spirit, seeing one another's difficulties and helping where they can, always remembering that it is a big thing they are planning and shaping, and not in any sense a personal or mean one.

Russia is distrusted by many—but if we know Russia, understand her, love her, Russia will know us and recognise our love. She will be quite easily amenable. She wishes a good settlement as sincerely as we do, but she is not going to be left behind if we or the French are going to be selfish and seek our own ends.

We ought to remember that commerce is a secondary consideration. If we get the right national peace, commerce will take care of itself.

And peace is not a primary consideration either. War will break out again—that is in the nature of the world. We must not be afraid of that. War has helped us back to reality now—it will help us or others again when necessary. Be sure at least we are not settling peace on national lines in order that there may never again be war. We are going to settle it on national lines because we feel that it is good to do so. As God made each new different living thing in the world and saw that it was good, so we shall save or resuscitate nationalities because it is fit to do so and will be good, being done. In fact, war becomes more likely the more

The Justice of Peace

little States there are. In a world of thousands of small States there is always a war going on somewhere—in a world composed of two or three vast Empires there is long peace. That is perhaps a debatable point, but the other point is not really debatable—we will make peace on national lines because it is just and fitting to do so. Our primary reason is that it is just, and that reason needs no help from other reasons.

ARBITRATION

THE signing of the Russo-American Convention was received with acclamation in the Russian Press. "Henceforth there will be eternal peace between America and Russia," wrote the Editor of the *Russian Word*. "Let us hasten to conclude similar treaties with other Powers—especially with Sweden and Norway, who feel so much in danger of our Imperial arm." I read in another Russian paper a translation of an article which apparently had appeared in the *American Outlook*. It was quoted with approval:—

"The time is coming when nations will become so civilised that they will not settle their quarrels by fighting, but will go together to an impartial international court and there await a verdict.

"Then, in such a case, a nation like Servia would be tried on the accusation of Austria, and the matter unravelled and blame allotted where blame is due, and a guarantee against new trouble would be obtained.

"The world will look back with astonishment on the barbarism of a previous age, when Austria could fall on Servia and take at once the rôles of judge, prosecutor, plaintiff, jury, and executioner."

" After the war," says another Liberal paper of Russia, "we shall look forward to a lasting peace throughout the world and the establishment eventually of the federation of Europe—the United States of Europe. That is what

Diplomacy is also a Kind of War

we are fighting for now—Peace and Federation, the recognition of private interests, but also the subordinating of private interests to the common weal, the recognition of nationality, but the subordination of national interest to European interest, to world interest. Such a trifling matter, as whether Russian Jews who have gone to America and have been naturalised as American citizens shall be allowed free access to Orthodox Russia, would not then jeopardise the lives of tens of thousands of fighting men in America and Russia. The inherent rightness of Russia's plea would then be made evident in court and the question would be closed."

A pleasant and a broad vista was disclosed in this article and one that would win a great deal of sympathy in the West. The war affords, no doubt, such exalted points of view.

Still, though I have stood myself and looked out over the new spaces of time and possibility revealed by the war, I do not see the world so smiling. I do not see it so happily parcelled out, do not see so far. I see mists and darkness between nations, rivers of blood between them, dark clouds of resentment overhanging some of them, pride and prosperity befooling others.

But to consider the fair Western vision as it has been described—What of diplomacy? Many aver—and among them he who most of all has a passion for shattering the world to bits and then remoulding it—

nearer to the heart's desire

that this war is going to make an end not only of war itself, but of the diplomatists. But it seems to me that even if it were likely that wars would cease, that very fact would increase the number of diplomatists. Diplomacy

is the way of arranging difficulties in time of peace.
Diplomacy is verbal and social strategy. One might as
well say that after this war we are going to get rid of
literary agents, lawyers, cabinet ministers, matchmaking
mothers and our capable selves. We are all more or less
diplomatists. Diplomacy fills the time of peace, and when
war comes, either national or private, it is often as a
relief, a release from words, politeness, flattery, deceit.

Some people speak of arbitration as if it were a blessed
dispensation of Providence, a means of finding Divine
justice and equity. But as a matter of fact the process
of arbitration—diplomacy, is also a war of its kind, a
struggle between astute men with white hands and silk hats,
a deadly struggle for the furtherance of personal ends. It
is not the baaing of lambs on a hillside. Nations will
still *win* their case by arbitration, for diplomacy is also
force. Some nations are strong in diplomatic gifts like the
Jews and the Russians, others are weak like the Germans
and the British. The Russians, for instance, are so gifted
that, despite a superficial aspect of frivolity and nervous-
ness, they may always be backed to come out well from
diplomatic struggles. No, it is not Britain's rôle to trust
her destiny to conferences. If conferences must occasionally be, let them be few and simple. Simple national
demands enforced by national power and national moral
right are what we must make, and we must make them
direct. If wars turn up occasionally it will be better to
bleed for a cause and an ideal than to be slowly bled away
by smiling foes. We shall not need to fight often if we
show ourselves strong and generous and kind, if we
assume the good will of the world and let our flag stand
for fairness, honour, good sport, good life.

The verdict of arbitration can only be acceptable as

the light of pure reason, and it cannot be a pure verdict as long as the representatives of the nations are backed by immense armies and unlimited wealth.

When the fortunes of the present war are made clear, the party that knows it is beaten may as well resign, and, of course, *pourparlers* of peace will be exchanged. When some basis of settlement that can be profitably discussed is found, there will be a conference between the representatives of Germany, Austria, and Turkey on the one hand, and Britain, France, Russia, Belgium, Servia, and Japan on the other. The scheme for belligerent Europe and Asia will then be put forward in a direct form. The broad principle of settlement will be indicated at the outset—that is, I presume, the national principle of historical territory to the nations to which the territory nationally and historically belongs.

It seems to me there will be no need to ask non-belligerents to vote upon the matter. America, Italy, Sweden, Holland may want fingers in the pie. America especially, as the only first-class Power not fighting, may be expected to claim the right to be a party in an arbitration conference. I trust not. There is a strong feeling in Russia, in Great Britain, and in France, strongest of all in France, that America be kept out of it. She is not yet a nation, she is a cosmopolitan crowd without any real unanimity or national self-consciousness. Her interests, moreover, are fundamentally commercial. In America, as nowhere else in the world, "money talks," and we do not want money talking in this matter. Despite the supposed advantage of Anglo-American sentiment, I would strongly advise that the peoples of Europe settle what is going to be done in Europe themselves.

But, of course, I am told, America won't be asked

to meddle in it. The answer to that is:—Germany will ask that America's offices be called in. Germany has had an eye to that from the beginning, and has spent an immense amount of money in order to obtain an unfair advantage through America's partiality. She has not failed in her propaganda in America. It is even part of German-American policy to make England think that she has failed, and that the whole of America is hilariously on the side of the Allies. We could not in honour accept the arbitrament of a nation that claims its right to arbitrate because it is *on our side*. We cannot accept the arbitrament of a nation that gives hospitality to the paid agents and propagandists of the other side.

But Germany will put her up as a necessary impartial voice in the conference after the war. But let us make up our minds to it now—those who have fought and those only shall decide the terms of peace; those who have not fought may formulate recommendations and send them to the conference, but they shall have no casting vote—no vote, in fact, at all—in the deliberations.

THE FUTURE OF THE RUSSIAN EMPIRE

WHEN the war is over and Germany is laid low, two Empires will stand facing one another, a land Empire and a sea Empire, two Empires and two peoples, the Russian and the British. The spectre of the German in complete armour has depressed us both, and caused us to think little of ourselves. But with the disappearance of the spectre we look at one another and see ourselves as we really are.

Even as the war goes on the greatness of Russia becomes more and more apparent, as if a mist were lifting off great mountains. Russia is emerging, and she looks so vast that it tires the eye to look over her.

We see her plains and her forests and her mountains, her ploughed fields, trackless woods, great hills, the majestic Caucasus with its long line of everlasting snow, the pretty birch-covered Urals agleam with precious rocks. We follow her great and tranquil rivers, the Volga flowing south, the melancholy Petchora, Dwina, Obi, Yenisei, Lena flowing through forests to the Arctic. We see the lakes and inland seas that she encloses. We see the endless steppe awave with boisterous prairie grass, and we look over the vast Central Asian background of salt deserts gleaming with crystal, of the irrigated yellow fields of Turkestan and Seven Rivers, away to the Mongolian trade routes, where the wealth of China issues forth in caravans of thousands of camels, away to the Great White

Russia and the World

Ones, the Altai Mountains, the backbone of Asia, we look along the wild Chinese marches where the Siberian rivers rise, where hundreds of miles are common as leagues in other continents, away to the far Pacific. Or northward the eye ranges over Siberia, and the great Northern Empire becomes visible, fringing in ice and snow a third of the way round the Pole.

On this wide world of the Russians live all manner of tribes—Russians, Poles, Jews, Finns, Georgians, Ossetines, Cherkesses, Kirghiz, Kalmouks, Shamans, Dunkans, Turkomans, Sarts, Afghans, Tartars, Ostiaks, Yakuts, Zirians, Samoyedes, an innumerable diversity, various in religion and tongue and dress. And one of the most remarkable and least remarked facts about all these tribes is that they are distinct. They do not intermarry, they preserve their own tongue and their own religion. They live as they please. In Russia the races are purer than in any other land in Europe. The Russians themselves are a remarkably pure type. Russianisation scarcely ever means the forcing of tribes to take on the semblance of Russians —it means occasionally the forcing of other races to obey laws they do not want, or it means, as in the case of the Kirghiz and Kalmouks, the loss of traditional pasture grounds, given to new-come Russian settlers, but it means nothing so deadly or systematic as Prussianisation. Under the crust of bureaucratic or absolute rule there is in Russia a remarkable freedom, even a spirit of Liberalism. Thus, the Tsar has several millions of peaceful Mohammedan subjects, and they are never interfered with even by missionaries—the Government even grants them facilities for making the pilgrimage to Mecca, and treats them more as if they were a branch of their own Church. There is freedom of religion in Russia, and Baptists and Evangelicals are putting up new chapels in every city. Even the Skoptsi, the celibate sect that believes that mankind, by having no children, should come to an end, are allowed to flourish, and nearly all the shops in one street in Moscow are kept by them. In Russia each caste is distinctive; you do not need to ask a man whether he is a peasant or a workman, or a Tartar or a Jew, or a Caucasian tribesman or a Kirghiz. It is at once obvious by his distinctive dress.

But Russia's greatness lies not in her government, nor in her national efficiency, nor in the army she can bring forward, nor in the inexhaustible resources of her country, but in her people, in her great strong human family, in her deep roots, her widespread national life, her big religious men and women, and the plenty of space they have in which to live. The Russian people has racial youth, nerve, and destiny; nothing can effectually stand in its way.

As I have lately wandered across Russian Central Asia, from the Caspian Sea to the frontiers of Siberia and Mongolia, all that vast territory which is printed yellow on our maps and marked with vaguely wandering caterpillars for mountains and troubled worms and millepedes for rivers, I have a very clear picture of one of the youngest colonies of the Russian Empire.

It has become very real to me. It is up-to-date in my mind. When I make my map of the country I shall erase half the Oriental names printed on our maps and substitute Russian ones, shall mark in new railways, new roads, irrigation systems, lately discovered lakes and mountains.

Russia does not advertise her doings, and as yet the travel book is almost unknown in Russian literature. For English people wanting to find information about interesting parts of the Russian Empire there is nothing that the translator can put his hand to and translate. The educated Russians are content to live in comparative ignorance of their own country and their own peoples. Of all the newspapers there is only one that is well served with information regarding the Empire, and that is the *Novoe Vremya*, read by some hundred thousand people of the military, aristocratic, and official castes. Russia has not had clear sight of the enormous importance that her Empire has in the world. It has, therefore, been difficult for us to realise it—especially as half our attention was taken up by the German bogey. We have surmised with some distrust the military and political advance of Russia in the East. We have not read the homely word Colonisation under the bitter word Russification, nor seen the peasant pioneers going before military interference and giving a natural plea for imperial absorption. The great fact about Northern Persia, Western and Northern Mongolia and the inclusive regions of Transcaucasia, Turkestan, and Seven Rivers Land is that there is an incessant stream of peasant colonisation thither—like a river of men flowing out of the depths of European Russia. What is called Russia in Asia is ceasing to be part of Asia, and is becoming part of Europe in the political sense.

Whilst I tramped eastward, across Russian Central Asia, all the early part of summer, I was scarcely ever out of sight of the caravans of the Russian peasant pioneers. At night they camped on the open steppe, as I did, sleeping under the stars; in the morning, when the horses or oxen were put in and the caravan started once more, it was with eyes and faces towards the dawn.

The days were so hot that everyone was up betimes and the road was filled with traffic, whilst only in the east there was whiteness and over the rest of the sky the jewelled darkness of night. I was awakened regularly by the heavy lumbering of wheels, and looking to the high road saw the little patches of grey and black that were wagons moving away towards the pallor of dawn, breaking the silence of night with the peculiar grunting and cracking sound of heavy merchandise moving slowly and ponderously on creaking drays.

There were the carts of new settlers all going a thousand versts and more; there were the carts of traders who go to hawk their goods in the villages, carts with consignments of goods, native carts with 8-ft. wheels, carts harnessed to bulls, to oxen, to camels. There were strings of camels with merchandise; camels with mountains of sheepskins on their backs, and on top of the mountains men. There were whole tribes with their herds and their tents, the women all on brilliantly caparisoned horses, the men on undulating groaning camels.

We went from oasis to oasis. About every ten miles there was a Russian village, not a weary, sun-stricken collection of mud huts, but a real little Russian village, with white cottages and thatched roofs, with schools and churches and little shops—but how much more delectable than in Russia! First, afar, you saw a clump of green trees; then as you got nearer you distinguished ranks of green poplars—young, tall, regular, and lofty. Then you came to a notice-board that told the date of the foundation of the village and the number of souls, male and female, at the last census thus:—

KRASNOVODSKOE,
founded 1884.
Souls
500 male,
400 female.

The ratio was generally as five is to four. Then you

entered a beautiful shady village where the cottages had front gardens and roses abloom.

I found the villages an interesting contrast to those in Russia. In Russia the villages are in the clearings, and dense forest lies between; but here the land was bare of trees all the way between, and the villages were in little forests of their own growing. But, of course, none of the Russian trees—no pines, firs, birches, maples, but poplars, willows, acacias without end. Water ran along hundreds of gullies, and the ducks flopped about in them, and called to one another. The houses when you entered them you found to be thick-walled, cool, white, and astonishingly clean. The settled population was tall, strong, clear-eyed, and rich as Russian peasants go—but without any knowledge of what was happening in the world where newspapers exist. For the rest there was an air of smartness and newness as if all the people had new hopes —something of the spirit of America rather than of Russia. As the wagons all stopped at the villages and the colonists and hawkers swarmed into the little inns, there was always a great deal of life and merriment. But no one could stop long. The road called relentlessly, even at midday.

How hot it was! In order to make my siesta at noon it was necessary to improvise a tent, tying my green plaid to a telegraph pole and to various heavy stones on the ground, and getting thereby a patch of shade in which I could sit and wonder what the temperature might be. How thankful I was when a little breeze began to flap and ripple in the folds of my plaid thus stretched. The people on the road went on, heat or no. A Sart came past in a blue cloak and with a tinsel skull-cap on his head; he looked like a representation of the Chinese Emperor in a comic opera. Five soldiers came by in a

On the Asian Highway

native cart, the roof painted in sky-blue blobs on dirty cream, the horses with ten necklaces of blue beads round their necks and with dangling swishing brooms of red strings hanging from the high shafts and keeping the flies from the horses' sides. A native squatted on one of the horses and rested his flat brown feet on the shafts—the sun was nothing to him. The soldiers had evidently been discharged far away and had got to get home as best they could, and had clubbed together for this conveyance. After them came weary soldiers clumping along on foot, and then people travelling in wagons and post-carts, and lying fast asleep in them. Then colonists once more, and the endless line of dusty, worn-out, lop-sided wagons that looked like enlarged pictures of old boots left in the mud.

I pulled down my tent after an hour and got on a little way—to the next village. Before the village was a stream and a bridge. When I came up to it I found an enormous accumulation of carts all bereft of their teams —for horses and oxen had been let loose to graze—and under the bridge and along the river such a scene of Edenic simplicity and bliss as I had not witnessed since I went with the peasants to the River Jordan. I also had a bathe—a river with three feet of water is a rarity in these parts. Bright little tumbling river that rose in the mountains and went on across the high road to lose itself—not in any sea, but in the cruel desert, where it finally becomes nothing! So, here for us, afternoon turned to evening, with refreshment, and though the setting sun was still hot on our shoulders we felt night breezes fanning us in front.

We passed through ancient towns—all mud huts, ruins, mosques. The bazaars had been made into covered bazaars by tying ropes across the busy streets and spreading green willow branches across them. Here sat the natives at work at their trades, or lounging in their caravanserais, or waiting for *koumis* customers. There were falcons in cages in many of the little shops. Sarts on horseback came carrying their pet falcons on their wrists as they went.

One evening I climbed up on to a green tableland surrounded by rocky summits and snowy peaks, a fine romantic camping ground, and there I fell in with a band of rich emigrants going from Stavropol, in South Russia, to beyond Kopal. They had twenty-four ox-drawn carts and twelve drawn by horses, and in the carts were their household goods—tables, chairs, beds and bedding, agricultural implements, reaping and binding machines, ploughs, grindstones, saws, axes, even metal baths, barrels, guns, pots, and whatnot, in such miscellaneity and promiscuity mixed with mothers and babies, that it was touching to see. The oxen in their wooden yokes were fine beasts, and the emigrants tended them on foot. Every wagon was accompanied by one or two on foot, who flicked off the flies and encouraged the oxen along, sang songs, and shouted to one another. Every wagon had buckets swinging at the side. One wagon had several cages of doves fixed on to it; to another a poor old dog was tied and came along unwillingly. In short, everything they could bring from Mother Russia to the new land the emigrants had brought.

"How long have you been on the way?" I asked.—"Fourteen days in the train and twelve on the road," a boy answered me. "How many days to go?"—"Thirty, perhaps."

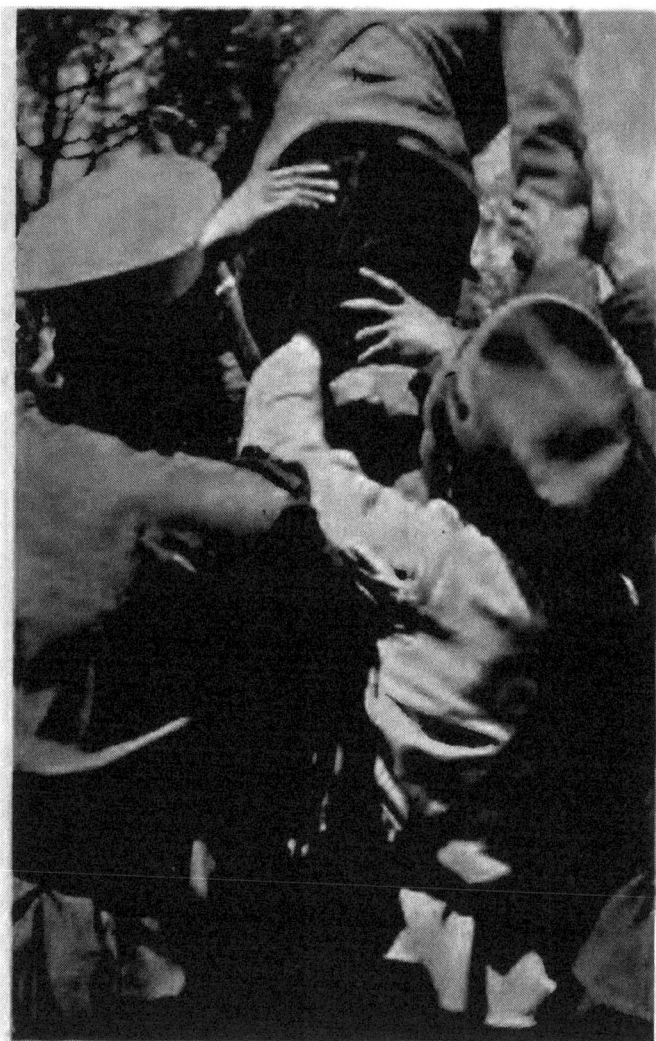

Hoisting the Ataman at the mobilisation. The
Cossacks also came to the author and said:
"*Pozvoltye vas raskatchat*—permit us to
give you a swing."

Emigrants on the Way

I had been much astonished to see a drunken party in one of the villages as I came along—a score of men, young and old, all with their arms round one another's necks and singing frantic tunes. I took it to be a wedding, but was mistaken, for I afterwards found it belonged to this party of emigrants. Presently a cartful of drunkards came rattling past me at a furious rate. They were all singing the Church Service, one in a red shirt was trying to keep time with his hand, another was astride the side of the cart and had one leg in and one out, an old greybeard was sitting with his back to the horses, and a young man was sitting down among the other people's feet. In the cart was also a little girl—somebody's darling. They went along at a terrific pace, and as they passed me, despite their bawling, I heard one man say: "No! Wait a bit, you've not got it right." But no one paid any attention to him, and the hullabaloo went on—"Yaoh, yaoh, yaoh, yu, yu, yohihoah . . . Yu."

They caught up the main body of ox-wagons and held a parley with one of the young women tending the oxen, but were evidently rebuffed, for when I caught up, the old man was saying, "I said we were fools, we were making a mistake ; great fools." Saying which he was pouring out glasses of red wine from a half-emptied gallon bottle and spilling as much as he poured.

"Do these dear drunken fellows belong to your party?" I asked of the boy with whom I had fallen into conversation.

"Yes, ours. They are all that are left. Many have fallen behind, and they will have to hire carts if they want to catch up."

Russia and the World

"Are you all going to Kopal?"

"Yes. No room to live in Russia. We have been trickling thither from our part for a long while. Many of ours out there—many."

"Have you got land out there?"

"Yes, we have taken land. We sent a man out and he has found us good land, and all our people are going, young and old. Nobody remains behind."

He, in turn, asked me whether I was going out to work on a farm or going to buy land or what, and I told him as best I could, and he told me to put my pack on one of the wagons, for it must be heavy. "All the same," said he, "on foot or travelling with oxen, you have got to walk nearly all the time. But it is not good to have a weight on your back as well."

After this for many days I was in sight of this caravan of wagons, watched their progress, and had many talks, sometimes resting my pack with them, but more often falling behind or going ahead of them. At night I spread my plaid near them, watched their fires light up, listened to the frequent crack of the gun—for they shot any bird or beast they saw and consigned it to the evening pot—was lulled to sleep by their Russian songs, and eventually wakened next morning by the roll of their wheels on the road. The drunken ones, I may say, gradually caught up and became sober. They took their places beside the straining beasts of burden, and let the others rest in the canvas or bast-shaded wagons. One morning when a wheel broke, behold the old greybeard, axe in hand, busily at work at repairs.

One day in the heat of noon we came to a little

brook, and so overwhelming was the heat that the whole long procession came to a standstill, and the oxen were let loose on the moor. They were furious with thirst, but would scarcely look at the water, so shallow and muddy was it. They were loose in pairs with their necks still in their wooden yokes, so it was very difficult for them to lie down or get rest. They began to try to gore one another, and to bolt, and for three or four hours the emigrants tried in vain to pacify them, and bring them back to the shafts. On another occasion we went some fifty miles without coming to a house or a stream or a bit of shelter, and our sufferings were all rather heavy. Such is the way of the road. Such is the way of the pioneers of the Empire.

The Russian Government controls the stream of emigrants and defines precisely where colonists may go and where they may not go. It dams a river and deflects the water through a stretch of country needing irrigation, and that done, lets the stream of people follow the water. It marks out plots of land and plans villages all in advance of the arrival of new-comers who will occupy them. Even so, nothing is left haphazard; the prospective settlements and farms are booked in advance, and the colonists travelling the long road with their wagons and effects have no hunt for land in front of them; they are going to definite places which they have agreed to occupy. We travelled from valley to valley with songs and hopes as to the promised land—land promised by the Tsar, and a ten- or twenty-pound Government loan with it into the bargain.

Alas, not seldom it is not twenty pounds, or two hundred, or two thousand that would suffice to start a

family on the land allotted. The colonists on the road
nurse a happy dream—they are going to Eldorado, the
future lies in their minds all glimmering in rose and
gold. The sight of the prosperous villages they pass
through confirms them in the belief that they are going
to a land three times as rich and happy as that they have
left. But often at the end of the way awaits them a
dreary, treeless stretch of barren sand. The great shady
villages of Syr Daria have taken twenty or thirty years
to build up, and they started in better country. Even
on the best virgin land immense labour is necessary, and,
as I say, it is often a tract of desert that has been chosen,
and no amount of labour would suffice to make it blossom
as the rose. Fifteen per cent. of the emigrants return
home to Russia empty handed, all lost.

Legally they have only themselves to blame, though
indeed they are more inclined to say it is the will of
God than to blame anyone. The Russian Government
invites no one to emigrate to Central Asia or to Siberia.
That is the first sentence of the Government handbook
on emigration. But seeing that there is "no room to
breathe" in some parts of Russia, and that the people
are always moving outward, it takes upon itself the
duty of regulating the movement, and providing all the
help and protection for the colonists that is within its
power.

But, needless to say, the voluntary colonisation of
distant parts of the Empire is extremely advantageous to
the Russian Government in the furtherance of its political
designs; the Government encourages the emigration of
Russians to the very frontier lines, and even over the lines
into Persia and China, and on the pretext of defending its
interests lends its military power to the extension of its

The Peasants' Forerunner

unnecessarily large dominion. The Russian Empire is vast, fertile and empty, but its southern and eastern limits are marked by a crust of colonisation. For instance, in the whole extent of Russian Central Asia it is only to the frontier of China that emigration is at present allowed. There is a long slender line of colonisation to the city of Verney, just a gossamer thread of villages, and then all about Jarkent and Kopal and Lepsinsk plots of land and prospective villages in abundance. Nothing that is less than 800 miles from a railway station is offered to the colonists.

If a Russian family wishes to emigrate, the Russian Government insists that it send first of all a messenger—what is called in Russian a *Khodok,* one who walks. The *Khodok* is allowed to wander about and compare the plots of land offered by the Government and make a choice. He is obliged to have a stamped certificate from the family he represents, and he has then the power to take land in the name of this family. One *Khodok* may represent three families but no more, so they generally set out in twos and threes, since the Russian peasants are inclined to emigrate in numbers, almost in whole villages. Needless to say, these messengers are sometimes stupid, sometimes adventurous men, who either select an absurd portion, or who disappear and never return. But most of them are level-headed peasants who do the best they can for the families who trust them. In any case, the responsibility is great.

The land being taken and the messenger returned, there is necessarily great excitement and hubbub in the village—and no doubt some repentance here and there. The families have to face the realities of voluntary exile, the parting with old faces, old scenes, the village church, the graveyard where their dead lie buried, Russia herself. They have to abandon their old cottages and sell at a loss many things that it would be folly to take with them. They have to pack their goods to take away, to see their live-stock bestowed in the cattle trucks, and get proper receipts for everything the railway is taking for them. For twelve roubles (twenty-five shillings) the railway will carry a ton 1,500 miles—a penny a hundredweight per hundred miles. They book their goods to the railway station nearest to the land they have taken, and take tickets for themselves in the emigrants' train.

There are special rates for colonists that would astonish the comparatively obstructionary Canadian or American railways. The greatest distance you can travel straight on by rail in Russia is greater—something like 7,000 miles, the distance from Odessa to Vladivostock. But such a journey costs only thirteen roubles or twenty-seven shillings—say, seven dollars—and in order to reach the vast emptiness of the middle West and far West of America it is necessary to pay between five and twelve pounds railway fare from New York. The following is the Russian rate:—

500 versts, i.e. 375 miles	1 rouble 40 kopecks = 3 shillings
750 ,,	4/6
1,500 ,,	7/-
3,000 ,,	12/-
6,000 ,,	24/-

So the price of a railway ticket is very little hindrance to the wandering of the Russian emigrant. The land they take at the end of a journey is given them free and is made their property under certain conditions. Loans are made according to the portion of the land and the difficulty of cultivating it. A hundred roubles in certain

A Paternal Government

districts near Verney and Pishpek, two hundred roubles in the rayons of Kopal and Jarkent. A hundred roubles is about ten pounds. The loan is made to the family and is returnable in fifteen years. The first five years nothing is paid back, but after that a tenth has to be returned each year. The Government is not, however, strict where a family is making a good fight for existence. In poor villages the Government takes upon itself the expenses of building materials for school and church— the colonists are recommended to give their labour free on "the work of God." Wells are sunk in places and roads made—at Government expense. It will be seen, therefore, that a great deal is done to substantiate the dreams of the colonists, and that where villages wither away and families desert their holdings and go home, failure is due to a mistaken original plan on the part of the Government surveyors and to a foolish choice on the part of *Khodoki*.

How different is the colonisation of the Russian Empire from our colonisation, and how different our Empire from theirs! What an advantage the Russian has in being compact, all on land, all within the grasp of a possible railway system, and liable to one spiritual and national nourishment on direct lines. Our people are separated from one another by immense seas. It takes much longer time and costs vastly more money to make a journey from one part to another. In our prosperity we tend to forget our essential unity, to let loose the ties of the motherland or the children lands. We tend to be just English, no more; to hold too narrow a conception of our race and function; whereas Russia, even in the days of failure and weakness, tends to be alto- gether, to be large but vital. If all this Russian space

217

Russia and the World

does fill up with Russians, what a collective voice Russia is going to have! What a bass!

But to return to the colonists themselves and to my impressions of them as I journey through a new colonial country. I have not been very much impressed with the life of the new land. The settlers are prosperous and healthy, their houses are larger, cleaner, and more seemly than in European Russia, but the spirit that really makes Russia interesting to us Westerns is lacking. Religion is on the wane and national customs are forgotten. Nearly everyone can read and write, but reads so little and writes so ill. The illiterate man may be as wise as Solomon, but the man who has learned to read has the whole long road of culture in front of him. In a land where there are no squires, no gentry, no *intelligentsia*, the colonist forgets where he stands with regard to his fellow men and to the world, and he quickly assumes that classes are divided by wealth and wealth only. The motto of the colonist is "get rich." There is little else in the life of Central Asia but the nascent gospel of "get rich"; it is full of cheating, swindling, harrying the Kirghiz and the Sart, colonial vulgarity and "bounce." As I read in the local pamphlet, "it flatters one's self-esteem to be rich"—a thought almost essentially American, and certainly far removed from the religion of suffering. It will be interesting to see whether the cultural barrenness of Australia and America is to be repeated in Siberia and Russian Central Asia. Perhaps not, seeing how much literary and artistic talent has been sunk in Siberia by the exile of revolutionaries, seeing also that the ever-increasing railway system supplies or tends to supply the colonies with the literature of the great European cities. Already the little city of

Claiming the Desert for Russia

Verney sends some thirty matriculated students to the university each year; at least, so I was told by a student whom I met at Pishpek, and with whom I journeyed part of his way home from Kief. And, having gone through a university course is not a mark of wealth or social position in Russia, it is essentially an educational distinction.

When I passed into Seven Rivers Land and beyond Verney along the Eastern frontier to Kopal it was touching to see the plight of the new settlers just arrived on their bit of land. Whatever hard word may be spoken of the established population must be withdrawn from these adventurous, much-suffering, much-hoping, much-believing people. All endeavour is blessed; all success is in a certain sense abhorrent; and we look with smiles and tears at the labours of pioneers, whereas we curse in one short word the prosperity which follows twenty years after the pioneers have achieved the heroic task of making a village where no humans have ever dwelt before. It is our heroic human way of thinking; we honour all attempting and daring and sacrificing because they reflect the God in man.

So along the Central Asian road human thrills are in store for every educated man observant of the beginnings of life. Here the 1,000-verst road journey comes to an end. The oxen are unyoked and the camp is pitched finally; good Russian prayers are said and words of thankfulness that the long journey has come to its true and successful end; there are exclamations of gladness; the colonists kiss one another and promise one another new life; there are also grumblings, lamentings, scoldings of the messengers who have chosen ill.

First of all trees are planted. How pathetic to see the

long rows of three-feet high poplar shoots and willow twigs! A month on this sun-beaten road leaves no doubt in the emigrant's mind as to what is the first necessity— shade, shade. Trees are planted all along the main Government dyke. The colonist chooses the place for his house and he digs a trench all round it and lets in water from the dyke, and he plants trees along the trench. Then he buys stout poplar trunks and willow trunks and makes the framework of his cottage. He interlaces little willow twigs and makes the sort of wilted green slightly shady, slightly sunny house that children might put up in a wood in England. But that is only the beginning. To the willow house he slaps on mud-puddings. This is the filthiest work; he makes a great quantity of mud and treads it up and down with his bare feet till he gets the consistency he requires, and then with his hand he fetches out sloppy lumps of it and builds his walls. In a few days the mud hardens, and he has a shady and substantial dwelling and one that in an earthquake will swing, but will not collapse. His roof he makes of prairie grass, great reeds ten to fifteen feet in length and thick and strong, or of willow twigs again and turf. In his second year he has a little hay harvest on his roof. He ploughs his little bit of desert. He exchanges some of his oxen for cows. He strives with all his power—as does a transplanted flower —to take root. He looks forlorn. You look at his poor estate and say: "It is a poor experiment; the sun is too strong for him, he will just wither off and the desert will be as before." But you come another day and you see a change and exclaim: "He has taken root after all; there is a, shoot of young life there, tender and green." Along the road I noticed villages of all ages; of this year, of last year, of four years gone; of twenty years, forty years.

Comparisons of Statesmanship

*And I took shade now and then beside the deserted hovels
of those whom the desert and the sun had beaten.*

Russia and Russian Central Asia and Siberia are in
much more intimate relationship than Britain and South
Africa, for instance. The heights of the Mongolian
frontier are still Russia, and the colonists there are taxed
from Russia, send their annual recruits to the Russian
Army, are reached by land from Russia, and look towards
the great cities of the motherland, Petrograd, Moscow,
Kief, as towards their own great cities.   But our British
colonies are by no means extensions of Britain or of Europe.

An interesting comparison may be drawn between the
tasks of Russian and English statesmanship in the moulding
of the respective Empires.   The late Joseph Chamberlain
saw the British Empire as a great self-supporting, self-
sufficient unity, able to produce all the food and clothing
it required, not needing to import anything from non-
British countries.   He wished a large thing—not a collection of separated fourth-rate Powers making laws at will
one against the other.   He wanted the British subject to
be always conscious that he was an integral part of something mighty and wonderful, wanted him to reflect in his
soul a large consciousness, the sense of our whole vast
majestical domain, and not merely the narrow consciousness of a little self-despising overcrowded island or young
commercial settlement.   The consummation of such an
ideal demanded a great ocean service and a mighty navy.
England must remain, in fact, Mistress of the Sea, and the
salt floods that separate should in reality join us and be
our national high roads.   A great ideal—but it has turned
out to be more difficult to realise than the statesman
imagined—the sea has separated us and has been difficult

to bridge over. There has not been the cheapening of passenger rates necessary for a great interchange of populations; there has been no journalistic *entente* between any of the countries of the Empire. It has been difficult to "get across" to one another, in body, mind or soul. Only now, perhaps, are we entering into an era in which great measures will be taken for the unification of the British Empire.

How much easier the task of Russia, the only other colonial Empire of to-day! Her distant populations have not crossed the seas. They have never felt themselves to be separate communities with separate interests. Fares have always been cheap and time has never been valuable. No one except the political exile and the convict has felt cut off from Russia, and only among the political and penal population in Siberia has the idea of separation found any home. Only in the backwoods of Siberia there has been mooted the idea of some new "War of Independence" and of the foundation of a "United States of Siberia." There was that danger inherent in the policy of making Siberia the outer darkness of those who found no favour in the eyes of the Tsar. But even so, Radical Siberia is nearer to Russia than loyal Canada is to us.

Turkestan and Russian Central Asia are nearer still. There loyalty is supreme. No Radical and sectarian emigrants are allowed to settle there, and, above all, no one whose conscience will not allow him to bear arms. The Government has pursued a policy of making the population as military as possible. In the event of a Mongol or Persian inroad the Russian colonists could hold their own without the help of the regular army.

It is improbable that any Russian Government will

grant local self-government to Turkestan, Seven Rivers or Siberia—unless at some time a revolution should take place and a demilitarisation of the Empire. The whole vast territory from the Caspian to Kamchatka will be administered as an imperial and military unity. And whilst it is held together in the strong grasp of an autocratic Government it is firmly bound together in a unity of commercial interests. By a skilful manipulation of tariffs and encouragement of industries, Russia is making herself a self-sufficient Empire as far as necessaries are concerned. She has agricultural and dairy products and meat in abundance, as a natural foundation. She makes all her own sugar, manufactures her own cotton goods, is even on a fair way to growing in Central Asia her own raw cotton, enough to supply the mills of Moscow and Lodz. She begins to manufacture her own wool and cloth in sufficient quantity. She has her own furs, her own timber, her own building materials. She is mining more coal and tapping more oil, and will certainly gain in time a sufficiency of fuel for all purposes. What she cannot produce for herself is machinery for her factories, the knick-knacks which we in the West make by machinery, the luxuries of civilisation. But even as regards luxuries she is well off—having her own good Crimean, Caucasian and Central Asian wines, her own Caucasian tobacco, her own liqueurs, her caviare, her inexhaustible supply of game.

In order to visualise the advantages of the Russian Empire as compared with ours, it is necessary to take our dominions and colonies out of their places on the map and tack them together with Great Britain, and imagine Canada sewed on to our western coast and

Russia and the World

Liverpool on the Canadian frontier, Eastbourne on the South African frontier, Southampton on the Indian, Land's End on the Australian frontier, trains taking only twenty-four hours to Toronto, only a week to Vancouver, thirty-six hours to Calcutta, sixty hours to Madras, twenty hours to Cape Town, twenty-six hours to Brisbane, five days to Perth, Western Australia, and imagine the interchange of peoples and of products, the circulation of our newspapers, the audiences of our books and Parliamentary speeches, the enlargement of our interests and of our imperial pride. How great would our Empire seem, how strong — immeasurably larger and stronger than the British Empire as we now visualise it, floated away into the distant places of the seas.

That is the advantage of the Russian Empire, that it can feel itself as Britain would feel in this imaginary picture of an all-on-land Empire. Despite the dream of separatists, Russia is not likely to give up this great source of strength—her essential unity.

My feeling, however, is that the Russian Empire is large enough—perhaps already too large. The Russians do not need to flood over towards Kobdo in Mongolia or towards the Persian capital. They tend to lose themselves out there. Russia wants an outlet to the sea, but the Japanese War has shown her that she is vulnerable at places like Port Arthur, as the Crimean War showed her that she was vulnerable at Sebastopol. Only in the centre of Asia or of Europe is she safe.*

The new railway to Verney goes on to Kuldja in China, and there is talk of its progression right across Mongolia to Kharbin. Undoubtedly it will cross China some time

* Opinion as to effectiveness of Russian army excluded by Censor.

or other and tap a great deal of Chinese trade. Already the Russians are strong on the Chuisky road that leads from Novy Nikolaefsk on the Siberian railway, through Barnaul and Bisk, Siberian river towns through Kosh Agatch, the Altai frontier station, on to Kobdo in the heart of Mongolia. Great efforts are being made to capture the brick-tea trade and indeed Mongolian trade in general. Russian influence is so strong that Mongolia is in the nature of an extra colony—something that must necessarily be taken over by the Russians later on. It seems to me, however, they do not need any territory beyond "The White Ones," as the natives call the Altai, beyond the Ala Tau of Kopal and the great heights of Pamir. Within these natural boundaries they can evolve an unexampled prosperity—if that is what they wish.

The Russian Treasury lost at least £50,000,000 per annum by the vodka prohibition. It lost another £50,000,000 by the cessation of imports and the consequent failure of import duties.*

Many new taxes have been introduced. Postage has been raised. It now costs twopence halfpenny to send an inland letter instead of, as formerly, a penny three-farthings. An extra ten roubles (one pound) has been charged on telephones. The income-tax has been raised. New State lotteries have been issued. An extra tax has been levied on sugar, on matches. A tax on bread and on kerosene has been suggested. But Russia cannot readily right herself in that way. She is a spending country. Everybody in Russia likes to spend; economy is very foreign to her temperament.

Still Russia's power of recuperation after financial

---

* Here followed 22 lines on the financial situation of Russia excluded by the Censor.

Russia and the World

exhaustion is very great. The great mass of her population is peasant, and it works for a half or one-third of the normal European wage. One or two good harvests and Russia is on her feet again, and all Europe feels well as a reflection of Russian well-being.

That is Russia's function, to supply Europe with bread. Even in war-time when all the youth has gone from the villages the fields are sown, women sow them, and if the war lasts over summer women will reap them and women will sow them again—women and children and old men. And when the war is over and the guns have been gathered in, the young moujiks and the Cossacks will return and give their arms to the work—and children will grow up and more children will be born. So

> green earth forgets
> The new-born generations mask her grief.

There is no new future for the Russian peasantry except a little modification in their methods of cultivating the soil and in the implements they use. The great health of Russia will lie in the peasants remaining peasants. I would utter a warning to those well-wishers of Russia who think that it is necessary to educate the peasantry, and who sigh for a greater exploitation of Russian commerce. It is this: that if you educate the peasant, he will cease to want to plough; if you dangle before his eyes the tawdry recompenses of life in an industrial settlement, he will be tempted away. The peasants are happy on the land, thanks to the satisfying popular rites of their religion, thanks to village customs, village songs, village sociability. Do not pervert them *en masse*. They leave the land in quite sufficient numbers to nurture with their elemental instincts and knowledge of mother earth the universities and the arts. It is a barely credible fact that even to-day Russia is falling out of cultivation, and twenty per cent. more of her land is covered with forest than was in 1860—owing primarily to the liberation of the serfs; secondarily to the lack of interest of the landowners in their own estates; and thirdly, to the lust of the peasants for industrial life.

Russia will be exploited commercially as never before. We can be sure of that, whatever her harvests are. She will be too pressed for money to resist that exploitation. If the English and French and Belgians are clever enough, Russia and Siberia will become their exclusive field. Russia has a great deal to gain by friendly co-operation with these peoples. She need not, indeed I think she will not, throw open her broad lands unrestrictedly to commercial and mineral exploitation. But she is likely to grant many concessions.

For my own part, I view foreign exploitation with a great deal of apprehension. It has reacted very badly on the lives of the peasants, whose best function, as I have said, is to grow bread. It creates a growing discontent in the minds of the workmen—always badly underpaid, if wages be compared with either Western, European, or American wages. It is not educative; on the other hand it increases immorality and vulgarity and has a subtle influence for evil upon whole countrysides. Take the life of the foreign mining experts, agents, engineers, managers, foremen, sent out by wealthy corporations to their Russian estates. They are princes of Russian travel. They pay the biggest fares, the biggest tips, live in the best rooms in the best hotels, make the grandest meals, those reserved and silent men, apparently uninterested in the lower life around them, the men who sit in proud isolation in first-class carriages reading "John Bull" or "Answers," or the French or Belgian equivalents, scarcely looking out of the windows; or, if they are confronted by a native, eyeing him with a sort of sportive mirth as if he had escaped from a show; giving importunate beggars silver, paying anything that is asked or that they dream fitting to whomsoever appears to have a claim upon them. When they get to the mine or the factory they meet their confrères, and grumble at the lack of comforts and the supposed ferociousness of the natives; they order from distant cities fruits, teas, biscuits, wines, what not, and pay double prices for food, lodging, cooking, service. They go about with revolvers in their pockets, pay bribes to the wrong people — paying more than they need, and teaching the corrupt to expect more and to demand more. They teach the peasant workmen, through their own fear, to think of murder and robbery, teach them to ask higher tips, encourage them to grumble about wages—and then, when a vile state of affairs has been created on a countryside, they suddenly receive orders from home to commence an era of retrenchment, and they begin to reduce wages and fight strikes—seldom retrenching in their own expenditure.

There is one great hope: it is that sobriety will make the peasant workmen stronger. Where vodka shops have been closed they are in many cases to be opened as schools. Once the peasant has become a workman and a sober workman he ought to be set upon the long road of education. The Russian Government ought to safeguard the education of its industrial communities. High ideals should be set before the workmen and their children. They should be made to feel that

The Peasant a Noble Type

learning and understanding are as long as life—are indeed life itself. It is rudimentary education and the *Universal Panorama* and short cuts to knowledge that are dangerous. The Russian peasant, become a workman, is capable of great development. From the peasant you can breed a noble type, witness Shaliapin, the kingly actor and singer, once a dock labourer at Batum, now able to forget everything else and fill the rôle of Ivan the Terrible or of Boris Godunof. The Russian race is wonderfully pure. Serfdom seems to have been an accident. The serfs were not an inferior race or a different race. They were, in blood and spirit and instinct, the same as their masters. The peasant to-day, cultivated and carefully bred, would make a typical Tsar. Nevertheless, as I said, do not think of educating the peasantry *en masse*. Millions would halt at the perilous halting places on the long road of education, and would so go to perdition.

THE FUTURE OF THE · BRITISH EMPIRE

THE wounds in our trade, in the ordinary course of things, are all waiting to heal over and be as before. After the war comes a period of convalescence, a becoming normal, a going-on. But England must not be allowed to fall asleep again. We must have a great England, an ideal, worthy of that vast number of people who speak our language and share our culture and traditions. Britain must realise herself as true mistress of the seas—hospitable mistress. Let us live more on the sea!

Russia and Russia's future suggest many things. And we may look towards Russia in order to see ourselves better. Though I do not suggest any rivalry between the British and Russian Empires, I do think we should do well to compare ourselves and learn what we can. The road is clear before Russia; she is an all-on-land Empire, and all she needs to do is to build more railways. That is simple, and indeed everything is simple for her. She is always a unity, always organically bound together as one thing, and she is going to have great advantages from that unity and from the simplicity of her problems.

Our destiny is on the sea. Our future is all problems, the sea itself being a problem. We also have to become a unity, not so much a unity of colonies, a unity of land painted red on the map, as a unity of peoples. We must not continue our policy of letting things shape

Making Our Colonies Nearer

themselves haphazard and trusting to racial pride and colonial loyalty to keep us always together. We have to make things easier.

Our habit as Englishmen has been to concentrate our attention on the life of our little island and to ignore the life of the colonies as if it were something second-rate or third-rate. Even in this hour of need frequently we hear, in answer to such questions as, "Aren't the Canadians loyal?"—"Yes, too loyal," or "Did you find New Zealand loyal?"—"Oh yes, a perfect hotbed of loyalty." That is unkind to our brothers out of sight and out of mind, and it is bad for ourselves. It is not even a true sentiment, nor could it be really true.

Imperialism has been unfashionable for a number of years, and the colonies have suffered by implication. We have given our colonists powers to look after their own affairs, and have begun to regard them as separate States. We have taken no care to give them spiritual nourishment, to give them the consciousness that they are part of something very large, that their small destiny is part of a much greater thing, our imperial destiny. And we ourselves have also learned to think small.

If we are to counterbalance the Russian Empire we must be large. We cannot balance two hundred million people spread over half the globe by sixty million huddled together on our little island. We have not the background, we have not a large enough thought in our consciousness. We must get altogether and be altogether.

What can be done?

The first thing that occurs to me from my wanderings in the Russian Empire is that we have to make the colonies nearer. We have got to think nothing of going to one of them and back. We have got to exchange readily thoughts, books, people. We have been more interested in the United States than in our colonies. In a sense, interest in the garish contrast of the States has come between us and interest in the people of our colonies. We have to realise that the United States is not really a kindred country, but a foreign country with foreign interests. For the rest, we have to make bridges to Canada, Australia, South Africa, New Zealand, India.

We need the Government to institute a State service of steamboats between the colonies and the Motherland, not try to make them *pay*, but to make of them public bridges between our far-off lands and ourselves. It should be possible for a British subject to go anywhere in the British Empire at a fare of about £1, and pay for meals as wanted according to a tariff.

Such an institution would be an immense gain. We have made transatlantic travel into a bit of snobbery. We have got to make the journeys on the sea unimportant and ordinary.

Quite obviously we diminished the cost of postage from a shilling to a penny in order that there might be a greater circulation of personal opinion and intelligence, and we had great gain. We diminished the price of newspapers from threepence to a penny or a halfpenny in order that we might have more circulation. It is all to our advantage, and much more to our advantage, to increase the circulation of the *people* of our Empire by removing the prohibitive prices that we have to pay in order to cross from one land to another.

The citizens of the British Empire want some privileges. They have not many more privileges at present than if they were Turks or Chinamen. We want im-

Going Forward in Love

perial confidence, we want to feel at home in the world and to go readily from one part to another. How greatly we should all gain by a quickening of our circulation and a sense of our organic unity, by feeling that the distant limbs of the body politic responded to the impulse of the brain and the action of the heart.

There is nothing to fear in the realisation of our Empire. Our days of aggressive Imperialism are over. We are ready to take over a desert here and there, or occasionally to organise the government of some tribe that cannot govern itself, but we are not going to enslave other nations or seize their land in order to exploit it for ourselves. We have more territory than we have people, or can have people for many a hundred year to come. We have to go forward in love, not in distrust or jealousy.

We look to those who come back from the war, those who have been touched by reality and the face of death, the great force that should come into our stagnant national life, bringing the quiet but potent thoughts dreamed out on the battlefield or sworn in the moment of danger and distress. These will bring their true passion to the making of the new life, the making of a good peace and the shaping of the future of our Empire.

NATURALISATION

THE war has raised in an urgent form the question of naturalisation. Have not the British been very slovenly and careless in their granting of the precious right of nationality? Why should Russians, Germans, Poles, Jews, Italians, and what not have the right to be considered British subjects, our own people? It is much better that Germans remain Germans to the end of the chapter. God made the Germans Germans as He made the black man black. German they should remain. Jews also should be Jews. In Russia a Jew becomes a Russian only when he gives up the Jewish faith and is baptised. In England also Christianity should be a compulsory qualification for complete nationalisation. Every man should have his papers of identity.

In America, of course, it is different. The Americans are not yet a nation—in America a nation is being put together and established. But in Europe the nations are formed, they are sharply defined. Peace when it is accomplished will be on strictly national principles. The territory that is really German will remain German; that which was French will become French again; that which was Polish will return to Poland. Therefore, the individuals in England who are really Germans should be made Germans again, and the Poles who are really Poles should be returned to Poland, and so on. If that retrospective view of individual rights is difficult to en-

Rights and Destinies

force, provision can at least be made for the future that nationalities may be purer and that Poles and Jews may be given passports of Polish and Jewish nationality, and that Germans be stopped masquerading as British.

The whole Liberal principle of the rights of individuals and of nations to be themselves and to realise their true individual and national destinies is bound up in this question of naturalisation. Liberalism is not chaotic freedom, but ordered freedom. It is true freedom. It not only sets free, but it safeguards. The compulsory cessation of promiscuous nationalisation is a great safeguard of the rights of individuals and of nations.

CONSCRIPTION

A HAUNTING question of the day is: Will there be conscription after the war? Before the war a powerful party, led by Lord Roberts and ministered to by Lord Northcliffe, wanted it, but the overwhelming mass of the people were against it. Liberals and Socialists were against it *en bloc*, many Conservatives, and also the man in the street. But the war has shown how great was the necessity for a large army. We have had to equip and train a million men in a terrible hurry, and have not had clothes for them to wear or guns for them to shoot with or horses to put under them. And now we realise that it would have been better to have prepared our army earlier, better for us, better for the brave men who go to fill up death-gaps in the line of our regular army.

Among Socialists have sprung up many conscriptionists, and Bernard Shaw is able to call for conscription for this reason—that since men may be forced to serve the State in time of war, they may also be forced to serve it in time of peace. He would have those men shot who in his opinion avoid serving the State.

Wells, on the other hand, wishes every man to be familiar with the use of the gun, and to be able to defend his home and his country-side whenever occasion arises. The working men and the discontented would then have material power when they were organised to

On the way to the point of mobilisation: 1,000 miles from the nearest railway station, 4,000 miles from the battlefields of Poland.

rebel.   Strikes would become civil wars.   The rich and those who are now powerful would find their position much less secure.   Incidentally, we should, of course, be much more formidable in resisting an enemy invading our shores.

The Quakers, the Tolstoyans, the Plymouth Brethren, and other quiet but none the less powerful communities are altogether opposed to the use of material force, and they could not be compelled individually to bear arms.   By English tradition we should be forced to grant exemption to those whose conscience forbade them to raise the sword.   The consequence would be that most of those who were not Quakers, but who for ulterior reasons did not wish to serve, would be converted nominally to Quakerism or Tolstoyism or the like, and would so escape, putting the onus and the handicap on to those straightforward Englishmen who did not seek to evade the hard year or two years of training.

But the question of whether we shall have a form of conscription or not is likely to become a deadly political quarrel before it can be resolved.   Liberals view with apprehension the coming of a military caste and the rising military contempt for civilians.   They fear the uniform, the sign of the sword, the distinguishing marks of the new military aristocracy.   They know that an aristocracy founded on military rank is more difficult to overthrow than the old aristocracy founded on estates or money or tradition.   They also say: Is not the German war the last war?   Did we not fight it so whole-heartedly because we felt it was not the Germans so much that we were fighting as war itself?   Has not our victory over the Germans been a victory over war?   Why, then, should we on the day of peace set out to prepare for wars to come, to attract by increased armies the fear and hate of other countries?

No one is likely to answer these questions. We know, nearly all of us, that the idea of a last war was merely one of the bluffs of the beginning of the war, a pretext, a recruiting fiction, something to fill green young men with a high moral fervour. It was wrong to say it perhaps, but it was said.

Alas, revenge is always heaping itself up! Material force is the insolvable quantity. Even in Britain, which has had the smallest army, and has prized peace most, the indignation of the people is put down with armed force, and we could not settle such a dispute as that between Ulster and the rest of Ireland without arming the parties. Hate is always gathering to centres and discharging itself. Nameless hate is in the air, and we capture it for ourselves and give it the name of our private quarrels. Even the pacifist *Daily News*, in the glut of national discord and fighting, summons Lord Northcliffe to battle, charging him with appealing to our lower instincts, whilst it itself is actually appealing to the fighting instinct in him, trying to get him to throw back words of abuse. There is a desire for fighting hidden in the breasts of everyone except a few ascetics and saints and poets in every nation, except in a few tribes of tent-dwellers, nomads, or cavemen. Under the crust even of America lies sleeping force, the desire and the need to burst forth and fight and devour, like the fire in the depths of the earth.

"What, then, of Christ's promise?" ask the Tolstoyans and the Quakers and the Plymouth Brethren. "What chance has Christianity of coming to anything?"

My answer is: every chance. Christianity is not for nations, it is for individuals. It is an individual under-

Glorious Imperial Service

standing. It is not a rule. It is a personal choice.
The peace that Christianity gives is the inner peace,
the peace in the depths of the heart even when the
outer world is full of war. In fact, the greater the
tumult of the outside world the greater is the miracle
of Christianity. · As the promise says: "My peace I
give unto you: *not as the world giveth, give I unto you.*"

The Tennysonian and Victorian—

> The Earth at last a warless world

is a popularisation of Christianity, and much easier to
give assent to, and to work for, than the truer

> The heart at last a peaceful heart.

But to turn from the individual back again to the
world, I think that when the war is over we shall indeed
set to work to maintain a larger army and give more
opportunities to youth to ride and shoot and perform
the manly exercises. We ought to popularise imperial
service and give facilities to our young men and women
to see the Empire,· and work for periods at different
points in it. We need to make imperial service more
interesting, we need to make it as interesting as it really
is. We need to say nationally and individually that
position in life is not the first thing, earning a living
is not the first thing, commerce is not the first thing,
that all these things are added if you have first the will
to serve an ideal. No compulsion upon individuals is
in keeping with the British spirit of freedom., But the
prospect of imperial service should be so glorious that
everyone should wish to come in of his own free will,
and Quakers and Tolstoyans who wished not to carry
the gun might still find an immense amount of scope

Russia and the World

on the positive side in the making of bridges and the
carrying of the messages of love and interest from one
part of the British Empire to another. Once more we
look to those who come back from the war to give us,
from their hearts, the wisdom which they have learned
in the hours of facing death for their country.

Last Thoughts

PETROGRAD

I HAVE been in St. Petersburg for the first time in my life, or rather I have never been in St. Petersburg at all, I have only been in Petrograd. Although I have been almost everywhere else in the Russian Empire I have always avoided the capital, expecting no pleasure there, no revelation of Russia. And wherever I have gone in Russia people have solemnly advised me that it would never be worth while to go to St. Petersburg, and they have rejoiced to hear that I never intended to go. As Merezhkovsky wrote: "The life of St. Petersburg is the death of Russia, and conversely the death of St. Petersburg might be the life of Russia." Behold, St. Petersburg is dead! Petrograd has taken its place. As the poet Aksakoff wrote:

> Its name was a foreign one;
> That's why we never remember it.

When first the new name was spoken it seemed annoying that it should rhyme with *retrograde,* but the pun was not apposite. The name St. Petersburg sounds sinister, grown old in sin; nothing sounds more childlike, young and simple than Petrograd.

The sun did not, however, shine on Petrograd for me, nor did the new sentiment transfigure the dreariness and sordidness of the great city. A moving mist was driving over the house-tops, and through it came a drizzle

243

Russia and the World

of finest snow or rain. The raw, penetrating air made one nervously cold. The streets were wet and slippery, and the wood pavements were old and worn and muddy. Every passer-by was muffled and silent. I went down the vaunted Nevski Prospekt, one of the greatest streets of the world. Its houses, shops and blocks are of unharmonised heights and colours, disorderly in bulk and in design, with no spaces between the houses, and with window-fronts greedily absorbent of wall. Such an anomaly as the Singer building, an American advertisement in stone, can find a place in the same road with the covered arcades that take their inspiration from the *bazars* of the East, and with great blocks of Government buildings the colour of fire-glow in the sky or of muddy water mixed with blood. It is a fine, long, straight, flat, wide street with electric standards along the middle, with car lines each side of the standards and red-striped trams pottering along, with diversified bunches of horse droschkies trotting forward, with coughing, swift-moving motor-cars, and antique baronial carriages having scarlet-clad coachmen sitting on their boxes. Bits of the street feel like Paris, bits like the East End of London, bits like Broadway, New York, but collectively it is something unique, something sinister and gloomy, brutal and out of date.

It is the city of Dostoieffsky's novels, the scene especially of "Crime and Punishment," and the nightmares of Raskolnikof. It is the scene of that wonderful tender novel "Injured and Insulted," the scene also of "Le Double," where a hypochondriac, leaning tired against a bridge over one of the canals, saw himself go past himself in the driving blizzard of snow. What sin there has been in this city, what meanness, sordidness,

~~St. Petersburg~~ –Petrograd

unhappiness! This hitherto half-German city! Sixteen thousand Germans were sent out of it in one week whilst I was there. St. Petersburg—Petrograd; yes, it is good tidings.

There has been a much stronger German influence there than in London. Germans at court, Germans in business, above all things Germans or naturalised Germans in the secret police. They should get rid of them all; denaturalise and disenfranchise those who are Russian subjects. They have been poisoning the national life. They are a great danger to the State. Their intrigues and machinations are words now, but if not checked might amount to actions later on. The Tsar's life is especially precious at this moment, not only to Russia but to England and France. He has come out unreservedly as the leader of his people and the promulgator of the war. He has trebled the strength of his army by the vodka ukase and by his consistently strong decisive personal behaviour. And all the while he has the haunting personal sorrow—the weakness of his heir. It is difficult to view with calm the presence at Petrograd of such men as the notorious Reinbot, once chief of the Moscow police. May the capital have a complete purge!

My eyes discover the dead St. Petersburg. I go to Vassily Island where poor Dostoieffsky lived in poverty. The dank and dirty water of the Neva and the canals suggests the suicide to my mind. But though the dead past is so evident the young present is also insistent. Petrograd is there. The spirit shops are sealed. Half the private-chamber restaurants are shut. In all shops and public places there are notices up requesting you not to speak German. Bright-faced young men and women dart about with picture post cards and news-papers, and call to you as you pass by, "Buy the news for warm clothing." At first you do not understand, but later you learn that the proceeds of the sales go to provide warm clothing for the men at the front. Then you understand the large placard everywhere exhibited, the touching reminder to the townsfolk of the capital. Everywhere you go you see the words

IT'S COLD IN THE TRENCHES

There are five or six new evening newspapers on the streets, and they are bought *na raskvat*, like hot pies. Crowds stand all day outside the offices of the *Novoe Vremya* watching for the new telegrams, which, as soon as they are received, are posted up. There is tremendous interest in the daily news, especially in the doings of the Russian Army and of the British Fleet. Away in the background somewhere the Tsar waits for news also, and receives it first of all before any of his people, and if it is great news he orders that it be given out at once. Then all the papers come out with extra sheets, and in the theatres the favourites of the crowd come forward and stop the orchestra. "One moment, one moment, please; a great victory in Poland. . . . God save the Tsar!"

RETURNING FROM RUSSIA TO ENGLAND

AS I had determined to return to London for a while I had to come to Petrograd. There I had to decide whether I would take the risk of the Scandinavian route, or whether I would go to Archangel and return on a New York liner that called at Liverpool. By most accounts the North Sea was closed, and there was no traffic between Norway and England except by boats going north of Iceland. However, the ticket agents averred that the way was still open, and I believed them, and they were right. Still, it was a most difficult and unpleasant journey, full of unexpected vexations and troublous doubts, relieved only by the hope and the coming joy of seeing my country again.

Into the fast Finnish train starting so late one night from Petrograd, and away towards the Gulf of Bothnia shore, the engine screaming like a sea-gull! The train runs all night long, and in the morning we emerge into a new country with a new landscape—Finland. A melancholy and yet beautiful country.

Snow-covered fields, cold wooden houses with pointed gables, red-painted châlets, an upland country on which Jack Frost has breathed. Vast shadowy lakes to which the lowering and tumultuous black sky leans down. There is a sadness beyond words, but it is a country to love tenderly. Far away lies the black other side of the lake looking like the end of the lake's life. We love

247

things that are limited—all mortal things like flowers, humans, little lakes—much more than we love stars, gods, seas. We are tender to all that dies, that has an ending or a limit or another side.

It is an individual country this Finland. The high white stone buildings, compact, many-pointed, bleak, are a reflection of jaggedness and ice. There is also a jaggedness in people's faces.

An accurate people the Finns, efficient, orderly, Protestant. They have their backs to Russia and look towards Germany and Scandinavia. One feels that they have a national destiny within the Russian Empire. It was worth while to get a glimpse of the people, if only on a two-day journey in their country.

We had to stay forty-two hours at Raumo on the coast—the port of embarkation for Sweden. We arrived at four in the afternoon, and instead of the train proceeding direct to the harbour it stopped at the town. We were informed that the three Swedish boats in the harbour were packed with Germans thrown out of Russia. We should have to go to an hotel. The hotels were all full; it was necessary to seek a hostess in a private house.

Next morning, while it was yet dark, we had to get up, hire sledges, and pelt through a blinding snowstorm to the pier, where a boat was supposed to be waiting for us. At the pier we found yesterday's steamer still loading and in no hurry to go out. A boat would come for us some time in the afternoon. Meanwhile our trunks were opened and all correspondence was seized and examined so as to prevent letters being taken abroad "behind the Censor's back." A boat came in and we were given cabins. Next day, about eleven o'clock in the morning, we steamed out of the harbour, led by a pilot.

What a boat that was! It was packed with German refugees from stem to stern. Germans on the decks, in all the passages, in the saloons and eating-rooms, crying, shouting, jesting. Directly we got out of Russian waters it was possible to buy lager beer and spirits, and the Germans appreciated the situation. As one old drunken fellow said:

"*Im Petersburg nicht wodka, nicht bier, nicht schnapps, nicht wein, nicht nitchevo niet.*"

All food and drink in the boat was, however, at starvation price, and the Swedes spoke no language but their own, and gave wrong change.

*   *   *   *

We arrived at Stockholm, a bright and stately city, at three in the morning, and submitted to the Swedish Customs. The German refugees were met by the representatives of their own nation and by a dozen motor-cars. They were packed into the cars, a dozen in each, and taken off to some Evangelische Mission to have hot coffee and sleep a few hours. At 4.30 a.m. the Customs closed and I took a taxi-cab to the locked railway station; after some banging I was admitted by a porter. The train to Christiania went at 8.38 a.m. This train had only second and third class compartments, but I travelled with two Russians who had booked first class tickets. We telegraphed to Christiania to reserve seats in the next train to Bergen, but arrived two hours late and had to spend the night at Christiania.

Christiania seemed a much dirtier city than London, if London were all East End. Its traffic is horse traffic, and the streets seem to be seldom cleaned. There was a pea-soup London fog and a penetrating raw air.

Next day, after a night in a cold hotel, I was informed that all second class seats in the Bergen train were taken. I had no objection to third class, so long as I got there; but I was rather amused to find that I must pay six crowns for a sleeping berth in the third class, even though I had a second class ticket. Next to me in this train was a Chinese British subject from Hong Kong. He had a first class ticket, and had paid something like £1 5s. extra for the privilege of going in a third class sleeping car. True, they had given him a carriage to himself. But then that rich Chinaman was tapped in an extraordinary way; money flowed from him like water at every place he changed.

*   *   *   *   *

At Bergen things were a little better. We all got the cabins for which we had tickets. But the more dangerous part of the journey commenced. The danger to civilians was a little heightened by the fact that we had on board five British naval officers and fifty marines, who had been wrecked off the coast of Norway, but had managed to leave the country as civilians. They momentarily expected the approach of a German cruiser, and, indeed, knew that there was a German submarine near Stavanger that had intelligence of their movements. At Stavanger they were all ordered to keep to their cabins, and not show their faces for a moment above deck.

It was rough weather. There were only three women passengers. We saw the noses of several floating mines. Many people slept in their life-belts, and we all balanced the idea of a sudden explosion, and a plunge into the

Dear England Once Again !

cold sea, or a rush to the boats. We were forty-eight hours on the sea, and the last morning was one of mist and fog-horns. British torpedo-boats rushed past us like monsters with their tails in the sea. Black torpedo-destroyers steamed round us. At last Tynemouth became visible like a shadow, the fleet enclosed us, a little boat drew up to us, and a man, with his hands to his mouth, cried out in a stentorian voice :

"Get your passports ready ! "

The Russians on board at once fumbled in their pockets for their passports. It was a familiar order to them. The British officers below, now in their uniforms, drank champagne. The sick recovered at the thought of England.

"Any revolvers, any letters you are trying to take past the Censor, anything to declare? What is your occupation? What have you been doing in Russia? What is your English address ? "

"You can go."

Yes. Dear England once again. Newcastle, the Scotch express. London, dark London. My word, how dark ! How difficult to get there from Russia !

Britain is great on the sea. All sea adventures touch us, and even the smallest details of the life of our men are interesting. How tantalising it is that the present vast activity of our fleet and the men on it is without its story. The only time when news becomes explicit is when we are told that a ship has been sunk and some of our brave fellows are dead. I have here a true story of one of the shipwrecked naval officers whom we took on board on my journey home from Bergen to Newcastle. It gives an idea of the strangeness and pathos and almost feverish activity of the lives of all our gallant sailors in this war.

On the first afternoon when I came aboard I was surprised to see among the passengers one Englishman wearing a Russian fur hat and another with an Archangel reindeer coat. There were several civilians who kept gathering in knots, talking mysteriously and then separating whenever anyone came near them. When questioned as to where they had come from they talked vaguely of the beauty of Mexico and then of the fiords, hinting that if there were light they would like to take some snapshots at Stavanger.

They were a captain and officers who had been on the ill-fated *W——* which sunk off the North of Norway, and they were disguised as civilians in case a German cruiser should come up and revise our passengers and cargo. Not until we had been twelve hours out at sea did they let us others know their story.

They had escorted the Canadian ice-breakers to Archangel, the ice-breakers that it was hoped would keep the Great Northern port open all the winter. At Archangel they had waited five weeks, always expecting to be returning on the morrow. At last they got orders to sail as passengers on the British tramp steamer *W——*. Seven days after leaving Archangel the captain of the *W——* entrusted his ship to an uncertificated pilot— the latter led them over a sunken rock.

It was at supper time, when everyone was gaily chatting and eating, that the crash came and the whole bottom of the ship went to shivers. Every one thought they had struck a mine. The passengers darted to their cabins and put on their life-belts, and stepped off the vessel into the ice and snow of the sea. A lighthouse

A Wreck

was near and they scrambled over ledges and let themselves down over icy precipices into pools of melting ice and icy water, and so reached the shelter. For twenty-four hours they shivered on this lighthouse and sent up rockets. At last a Norwegian post boat hailed them and took them off to Trondhjem, where they were at once put under arrest. Eventually they were allowed to return to England—thanks to the courtesy of the Norwegian Government. All the British naval men were saved, and not only they, but the captain's black cat, Tim. Tim was a great favourite on our journey from Bergen to Newcastle, and many of the sailors thought our safety depended absolutely upon him.

The officers were interesting Englishmen, gentle, calm and firm. I realised that in such men as they lay Britain's true strength. My especial friend of the journey was a young lieutenant who was most eager for England and the Empire. Above all things he admired Canada and the spirit of the Canadians, and he promised himself that when the war was over he would marry and settle down in British Columbia. I wish London would always remember that when one of her sons leaves her and goes to a place like British Columbia, he is not lost to Britain: he belongs to Britain even more out there than he could at home. His heart beats for her; his arm is ready at her service.

"We were off the shore of Mexico when the war broke out," said he. "We received orders to proceed at once to Victoria, B.C. I was very glad. My sweetheart lives there, and we have been engaged two years. I thought 'now is my chance, we'll get married at once.' But when I got to Victoria another order was awaiting us. We had eight hours in which to pack our things to go to Halifax. I saw my girl for just one hour before departure. But I thought 'Halifax is not far, I can come back and marry her.' But when we got to Halifax what was my astonishment to find that we were under orders to proceed at once to Archangel. It took my breath away; it was such an unlikely destination. I had barely heard of the place before. We escorted certain ships (the ice-breakers, I feel sure) to Archangel, accomplished the journey safely, and when we arrived at the northern port of Russia the Russian Government made us presents, the captain three hundred roubles, each of us one hundred roubles, and each of the men thirty roubles. Yes, they were very hospitable to us also, and it was interesting to see the life of Archangel, but we were all crazy to rejoin the fleet. We were put on the ill-fated *W——* and were wrecked, taken through Norway, and put on this ship. When we get to Newcastle we shall find new orders awaiting us. I hope to see my father in London. I've been three years away from home, and no one has the least idea where I am or whether I am alive or dead.''

How excited everyone was when at last we entered British waters, and the officers put off their mixed British and Russian attire and donned their uniforms of blue cloth and gilt braid. The ship hummed with boyish excitement. At Newcastle all the kit that the men had saved from the *W——* was brought up first, and the officers and men went off before any of the other passengers. The orders at Newcastle were that they should travel direct to London and report themselves at the Admiralty. A second order came directing that my lieutenant should not stay at London, but should go direct to Portsmouth and take with him the marines.

At Newcastle

I found him in the train from Newcastle. He was appallingly excited and tired, and had deep black circles below his eyes. "Isn't it hard luck?" said he. "I haven't seen my people for three years, and now I have to go straight on to Portsmouth. I was so pleased to think we were to be in London for some days. You know you can telephone from Newcastle to London. It costs three-and-sixpence, but isn't it a miracle? I rang up my father. Just picked up the receiver, put it to my ears, and called into the tube: 'Is that you, father?' I could hear the old man gasp, hear the shuffle of his feet. . . .

"'Is that you, my son?'

"'Yes, I am at Newcastle, just arrived, and am coming to London. . . .'

"What a sweet moment it was! And then I had scarcely put the receiver back again on its hook when I was handed the Admiralty telegram to the effect that I was to catch the 5 a.m. train at Waterloo, and not let the men out of my sight till they were safely bestowed in one of the vessels of the fleet. We have to keep a sharp eye on them, they've plenty of money and would be off drinking if they got a chance. . . ."

This, perhaps, gives a glimpse of the life of the defenders of our shores. Someone came into me the other evening and I asked, "What news is there?"

"Only a British warship sunk," was the reply. *Only!* And only a few hundred brave and loving and patriotic men like my lieutenant drowned, men with sweethearts and homes and an undying love of their country. Let us remember always that the Empire is in the hands of heroes.

So I find myself in London. My first impression is one of gloom. Business wishes to be as usual, but cannot quite manage it. The ragtimes have stopped; the barrel organs play national anthems instead. There is not so much laughter, not so many witticisms, many more serious faces. There is depression owing to the absence of news. Squads of mixed sizes of recruits go by in unwonted looking khaki suits and the passers-by give no cheers. Darkness at night, and the lurid eyes of the searchlights on the Thames.

But looking farther, I am aware of a great optimism and a renewed national vigour. The people who can really help England are at the fore; those who are frauds, self-seekers, mere self-advertisers, have fallen out. There is a brisk breeze blowing against the cobwebs of lazy habit. Forces are beating against the snobbism in our State departments, education, social life.

Thousands of people breathe a prayer of this sort: "I hope the war won't end till England has been thoroughly wakened up. I hope the war won't degenerate into a sort of triumphal procession for us. I only hope the Germans will keep their end up till we get a thorough shaking-up."

Everyone sees gain ahead for England if only the war be hard enough and long enough for us. Yet at the same time it seemed strange to me when I first came back to hear the opinions of Londoners :—

"It all depends on the Russians. We are waiting for *them*."

"We hold them on the Aisne; we shall starve them out."

"It is money will tell in the end; we shall finish them with silver bullets."

To which opinions I necessarily replied: "The Russians cannot do much yet on German soil. Warsaw is going to be in danger off and on all the winter. Directly the Russians begin fighting on German soil they are up against German science, German railways, German technical superiority. The Russians have a much harder task than the French and English on the other side. You must depend on yourselves if you are going to win properly. When once the hands of the Germans are forced on the west, Russia will follow heavily in the east. Everything depends on prosecuting the war with vigour.

"As for starving the Germans out, don't believe it. It is not likely. The Germans, with their extraordinary gift for organisation, and their accuracy and discipline, will easily organise their internal trade and their country of Germany (including conquered Belgium); and they can live in a state of war for a whole era like the Romans. The more time you give the Germans the more difficult it will be to crush them. They are a hard people ; there is little give in them.

"And as for winning by force of money, that is a poor, foolish materialism. Nothing can be won by money. It is almost a truism to say that men fight more courageously when they have lost everything. The more faith in money we have, the less likely are we to endure to the end."

A few weeks after I had returned, the absolute reliance upon Russia began to slacken, and a good new faith began to appear—faith in ourselves.

"If you want a thing well done, do it yourself, John !" and England began to prosecute the war with increasing energy, both on land and on sea. News of victory in Galicia was received thankfully, but was not regarded as having the peculiar significance of being likely to relieve the situation on the Aisne. I began to hear the true whisper : "We could beat them ourselves."

NOT TOO LOUD!

DOWN in our East End, in the sweated labour dens, women are busy making flappers and squeakers and tiddlers and feathers, and what not for the celebration of peace. Even German Jews are engaged in the business, and are making a considerable speculation upon our mafficking again. If peace is postponed too long, then these wares will be put forth on the occasion of great victories or the German evacuation of the Belgian cities.

There will be room to be joyful. Our populace will want to shout and get drunk and throw confetti about and make a great noise. And yet I hope the noise will not be too loud, and that those of us who are quiet-souled will not be too much upset by the clamour. If all the public-houses and off-licence places could be shut for a week during the peace celebrations, or on days when we rejoice over victory, I imagine the noise would be of a more tolerable quality. Perhaps, however, the sweaters in the East End are making a miscalculation. We shall be quiet in our joy. So many more of us this time will have lost brothers in the war, so many families will have the remembrance of great sorrow, and England will be in black.

Those who have perished will also rejoice with us in the victory and in peace. They will look down as the

The Day of Peace

stars look — serenely. A verse of Alfred Noyes gives the thought:

> " When the last post sounds
> And the night is on the battlefield,
> Night and rest at last from all the
> tumult of our dreams,
> Will it not be well with us,
> Veterans, veterans,
> If with duty done like yours we lie beneath
> the stars ? "

The day of peace is one when every man should go to Holy Communion and eat and drink the Bread and Wine of those who have suffered and died for us all, and so enter into communion with their spirits and their passion. Do not let them die or think that they are dead. Find them again, find them again !

We are accustomed to think of the Germans as coarse and brutal, and yet we may upon occasion learn tenderness from them. One of the most touching things I remember reading of the Germans was the way the news of the fall of Antwerp was received in one of their theatres. A political play called "1914" was being performed. It was about half-past ten at night, when suddenly the manager came on to the stage, interrupting the players and the orchestra, and crying out:

"One moment, one moment, gentlemen; Antwerp has fallen."

There was tremendous excitement among the audience, the waving of arms, cheering, shouting, singing, the singing of "Deutschland over all" and "The Watch on the Rhine." Then suddenly the manager came forward again and imposed silence by his lifted hand. Follow-

ing him came the chorus singing in a remonstrant tone
this beautiful song :

Nicht zu laut !
Nicht zu laut !
Denkt g'rad jetzt wo Ihr jubelt und lacht ;
Nicht zu laut !
Nicht zu laut !
Fiel ein krieger vielleicht in der Schlacht
Und er liegt beim zerschossenen Pferde
Und nimmt abschied von Mutter und Braut—
Nicht zu laut !
Nicht zu laut !

which may be read in English :

Not too loud !
Not too loud !
Think just now whilst you laugh and cheer ;
Not too loud !
Not too loud !
How out on the battlefield dark and drear
A soldier lies dying, his dead steed beside,
And bids farewell to mother and bride—
Not too loud !
Not too loud !

Which might also be the motto of our remonstrance and
our hope in the noisy hours of triumph. Not too loud!
There in the dust where the enemy is lying, but for the
grace of God England might be lying too.

PRINTED BY CASSELL & COMPANY, LIMITED, LA BELLE SAUVAGE, LONDON, E.C.
75·415

Ingram Content Group UK Ltd.
Milton Keynes UK
UKHW020032040523
421194UK00005B/67

9 780530 789026